W9-BUB-460

RAT

How the World's Most Notorious
Rodent Clawed Its Way to the Top

JERRY LANGTON

St. Martin's Press ❧ New York

www.stmartins.com

Library of Congress Cataloging-in-Publication Data

Langton, Jerry, 1965–
    Rat : how the world's most notorious rodent clawed its way to the top / Jerry Langton.—1st U.S. ed.
        p. cm.
    ISBN-13: 978-0-312-36384-0
    ISBN-10: 0-312-36384-2
    1. Rats.   2. Human-animal relationships.   3. Rats as carriers of disease.
I. Title.

QL737.R666 L345   2007
599.35—dc22

                                                        2007012961

First published in Canada by Key Porter Books Limited

First Edition: July 2007

10 9 8 7 6 5 4 3 2 1

For Teensy, Dida, and the H-Dogg

Table of Contents

Strange Bedfellow

In 1994, a 24-year-old woman went to an emergency room at a hospital in Hempstead, England. She was suffering from a high fever and a large abscess on the inside of her left elbow. She had no history of such symptoms and had no idea why she was sick. Doctors brought her fever down and drained her abscess, which showed traces of both streptococcus and e. coli. Four days later, she returned. Again she had a high fever and this time she had an even larger abscess on the top of her right foot. Eight days after that, she came back again, this time with three different abscesses. Extensive interviews revealed that she slept with her pet rat. Doctors suspected that the abscesses were the result of rat bites and local authorities confiscated the pet. The abscesses disappeared and the patient recovered fully.

Source: British Medical Journal

An Eating
and Reproducing
Machine

U nless you're huge, Ed is probably bigger than you. He's the kind of guy who has to duck when he goes through some doorways and sometimes has a hard time finding suits that fit. Now that he's a consultant and making some real money, that's become a bit of a problem. But the former college football player wasn't wearing a suit on the cold April morning when he went out to clean his garage. Instead, he was wearing the new blue-and-yellow Columbia ski jacket that he got as a gift at some corporate event. He knew it was too nice a jacket to wear to clean the garage, but it was cold out and the jacket was handy, so that's what he had on.

He'd only been in the garage once before, when he looked at the house before buying it. It was a mess, but it didn't make much difference to him. Ed was desperate to get into Toronto's skyrocketing real estate market while prices were still headed upward, so he took what was basically the best house he could afford. It had potential, but it also had some drawbacks. It was located in Parkdale, traditionally considered Toronto's worst downtown neighborhood, and it had not been well taken care of. The elderly couple who'd owned it before Ed weren't up to even the most basic maintenance and all their kids lived far away. The house was a dump and the garage was even worse.

But it didn't scare Ed. He was a hardworking guy who, without any help from anyone, had managed to parlay two years of college and his own natural aptitude, charm, perseverance, and twenty years' experience in sales into a successful consultancy. He was tough enough to put up with the rough neighborhood until the inevitable spike in housing prices forced it to change for the better. Until then he would do whatever he had to in order to make his little house habitable.

So, armed with a bucket, a bunch of cleansers, a mop, and a broom, he went into the garage. As soon as he opened the door, he heard the scurrying of small feet. Damn squirrels, he thought. Squirrels, in particular eastern gray squirrels, are everywhere in Toronto, as they are in many big North American cities. They're bigger and more aggressive than most other tree squirrels and are better adapted to life close to humans. When gray squirrels arrive, red squirrels (whose young are often eaten by gray squirrels) are usually forced out. Gray squirrels, which can be quite charming as they flit from tree to tree and beg for treats, were introduced to many European city parks shortly after World War ii. By

1970, they had driven out much of the local fauna and became pests. On both sides of the Atlantic, they are known to invade our homes and gnaw at our garbage cans, but are generally tolerated, even enjoyed, because they keep their distance and they are pretty cute.

But Ed was in no mood for a bunch of fuzzy-tailed freeloaders in his garage. He knew that nesting squirrels could cause major structural damage and, from the smell, he could tell that it had become the rodents' neighborhood restroom. "I knew it wasn't a long-term solution, but I acted on instinct," he said. "I'm 260 pounds, and a squirrel is what... half a pound? He should be scared of *me*. Even if I couldn't get rid of them for the long run, at least I could scare the shit out of them."

He grabbed his broom and started batting it at where he heard the scurrying. The garage had beams about nine feet off the ground and someone years earlier had used them to store a bunch of now-decaying cardboard boxes. Some were balanced on the beams themselves, others were resting on boards placed on top. Ed smacked the boxes. He whacked a stack of old newspapers. He smashed a roll of insulation and his entire life changed.

Nobody but the rat will ever know if it took flight because of the impact of Ed's broom or because it decided to jump for safety. He said that it leapt, as I've seen rats do, straight up, somersaulting in the air. It twisted its backbone in midflight, like a cat, to ensure a feetfirst landing. It landed on Ed's head.

It all happened too quickly for him to react. Maybe it jumped again or maybe it just bounced, but when Ed finally realized what was happening, the rat was in the hood of his jacket. Immediately, he tried to hit the rat with the broom.

For its part, the rat tried to climb out of the hood, but the broom-handle assaults probably prevented its escape. Ed ran out of the garage and into the alley. He lay down in a patch of grainy gray snow and rolled, hoping to kill the intruder. As Ed put his weight on his right shoulder, the rat squirted out, running into the shadows, looking none the worse for the encounter.

Ed freaked out. He couldn't sleep in the house that night and told me he's had rat-themed nightmares ever since. He threw the coat—originally worth about $300 but now with a hood full of rat feces—away.

We're sitting in a booth at a fast-food restaurant as he tells me the story and I notice he rarely looks at me when he's talking. He looks at his hands instead, reliving every little gesture, every parry and blow. It's clear to me that he's telling the truth because he's sweating even though it's cold in the restaurant. He's getting pretty intense, so I try to lighten the mood. Half joking, I asked him if he had to change his pants after the encounter. He turned and looked me silently, sternly in the eye for at least a minute. "Have you ever had a rat in your clothes?" he asked me. I couldn't speak; I just shook my head. Ed now lives in a town house in suburban Oakville.

Perhaps Ed was overreacting. It was only a rat, after all. Rarely topping more than a pound in weight, the timid rat hardly seems like much of a threat—some people even keep them as pets.

It's not as though Ed ran into a lion in his garage. Equipped with giant retractable claws, bone-crushing jaws with three-inch canines and a startlingly athletic 550-pound frame, a lion can run 50 mph and bring down prey as large as a 2000-pound cape buffalo with what seems like ease.

While an encounter with a single lion would almost certainly cause a human more damage than a confrontation with a single rat, those contacts are exceedingly rare.

Humans and lions cross paths infrequently simply because lions themselves are scarce. The few centuries in which humans have held sway on earth have been absolutely disastrous for lions. Ancient Greek historians Aristotle and Herodotus mention prides of lions in the Balkans just about 2500 years ago. And when the Persian king Xerxes advanced through Macedonia in 480 BC, he sadly reported that he lost a considerable number of his camels to marauding lions.

As humans gained in population and technology, lions became our competitors and sometimes our outright enemies. Requiring immense amounts of open space and eating basically the same animals humans favored, lions were squeezed, starved, and hunted almost out of existence. The range of the Asiatic lion, which once stretched from the Italian–Croatian border almost to Indonesia, has been reduced to a 200-square-mile reserve in western India with, at last count, 243 scraggly individuals. The African lion is doing somewhat better, with about 27,000 cats, almost entirely in parks and reserves. Though not quite endangered, African lions are threatened by habitat loss, poaching, disease, and inbreeding. If not for the dedication and tireless efforts of conservation organizations and a number of not entirely stable governments, the African lion could be wiped out in a matter of months, by nothing more than negligence.

Contrast that with the humble rat. Starting out near the bottom rung of the food chain in the crowded jungles of Southeast Asia, the rat has enjoyed outstanding success in the same timeframe that lions have been almost wiped off the face of the earth.

With a worldwide population that even conservative estimates place at many billion and most consider the highest of all mammals—including humans—the rat has conquered every continent except Antarctica (although they have infested a number of islands in the Antarctic sphere). According to Steve Belmain, a British scientist who probably knows more about rats than anyone else in the world, rats live everywhere humans do "with the exception of the scientific outposts in Antarctica, but those don't really count as the people are not there naturally. If humans naturally lived in Antarctica, I'm sure rats would live there too." Rats are a menace in the searing heat of East Africa, in the steamy jungles of Brazil, in the cool rocky meadows of the Falkland Islands, and in the frozen bogs of Siberia.

That extraordinary adaptability is the primary reason that rats have been so successful. The small, short-furred rats in the palm trees above Moroccan outdoor markets look like an entirely different animal when compared with the hulking, woolly rats you'd find around the Dumpsters behind fast-food outlets in Anchorage, Alaska. It really doesn't take long for rats to adapt to any environment, no matter how inhospitable it may seem. Rats live deep under the earth's surface in coal mines, surviving on what the miners leave behind. Colonies of rats have even been known to thrive in meat lockers, where constant freezing temperatures would kill humans in a matter of minutes. According to a study conducted by Michigan State University, rats adapt to refrigerated life by growing longer, thicker fur and an insulating layer of blubber from their high-fat diet, and by nesting inside animal carcasses.

Although all animals, especially mammals, can adapt to their surroundings, few if any do so as rapidly as rats. The reason behind this would appear to be the rat's amazing fecundity. Rats just love having sex and they do it all the time. Male rats regularly mate with underage and already pregnant rats and have even been photographed mating with dead rats, their heads still caught in snap traps. Sometimes, groups of all-male rats will have sex with one another.

If you see a female rat over the age of six months, she is almost certainly pregnant. Gestation lasts for about three weeks, after which a litter of between 6–12 (usually 8 or 9), pink hairless rats are born. And rats have developed an adaptation more remarkable than their love of sex or the size of their litters to keep their numbers up. The female rat's reproductive system is so simple—one of the reasons baby rats are so helpless and underdeveloped when they are born—that giving birth isn't a huge barrier to getting pregnant again. "The most important aspect of rodent breeding is a phenomenon called post-partum estrus," said Belmain. "This means that females rats can ovulate, mate and conceive within hours after giving birth."

Coincidentally, the rat's gestation period is about the same length of time as baby rats need to nurse. "A female nurses one set of young for twenty-eight days while

Growing Up Fast: Developmental milestones for rats

Teeth emerge	8–10 days
Complete fur coat	9 days
Eyes open	12–14 days
Travel outside nest	14–16 days
Weaning	20–21 days
Venture above ground	22–30 days
Puberty (female)	34–38 days
Puberty (male)	39–47 days

Source: David Pass and Graham Freeth, Animal Resources Centre (animalresource.org)

she is pregnant with another set," said Belmain. "The first set is weaned just before she gives birth to the next set. This would mean that a female could give birth to another set of young every twenty-eight days, never having more than one litter to look after at a time."

It's possible then, for a three-year-old rat to have given birth to forty-three different litters, up to 516 separate births. When her children, grandchildren, and great-grandchildren get into the act, it's possible for her to be responsible for up to 16,000 offspring in a single year, and the number approaches 100,000 if she lives for three years. Of course, those figures are under ideal conditions with plenty of food and no deaths to predators or other causes, but actual numbers are still staggeringly high. Such huge populations of new rats and their habit of inbreeding invariably result in all kinds of mutations, many of which thrive in what would otherwise be tough environments. In cold places, fatter and hairier rats are more likely to survive, mate, and pass on their genes than their thinner, less well-furred cousins. The net result is a population of increasingly blubbery and woolly rats. Of course, other habitats and conditions favor other characteristics.

But the adaptation that has helped rats the most has been their ability to live with humans. While most other non-domesticated animals go to great pains to avoid contact with people, rats seek us out. One reason they like us is that they like our food. "These rats are usually generalist omnivores—they'll eat anything," said Belmain. "They can eat rubbish, sewage, dead bodies as well as whatever they find in our kitchens."

But unlike lions, which challenged humans on the hunting ground and occasionally included them in their diet, rats are satisfied to take our scraps. Rats, acting more as an annoying parasite than a threatening rival, eat what we waste, misplace, store, or don't consider food. By being small and inconspicuous, the rat has largely fallen under our radar. Until scientists Alexandre Yersin and Shibasaburo Kitasato conclusively linked them to bubonic plague in 1894, rats were generally considered more of a nuisance than a threat.

Our homes provide them not only with warmth and shelter from rain and snow, but also from predators—other than ourselves and our pets, some of which have been specifically designed to get rid of them. But compared to hunters like red-tailed hawks, great-horned owls, and coyotes, squeamish humans, easygoing Labrador retrievers and well-fed house cats hardly present much danger. Humans can be a bit of a problem with their snap traps and poisons, but rats either adapt to these introduced dangers or die. Many will develop immunities to poisons or simply avoid them, instead taking food they know is safe. But sometimes, they will be killed, even in great numbers. If the environment will support them, however new rats—displaced from other places either by human effort or by inter-rat competition—will arrive to start the process again. There are always more rats.

There are more rats because they have adapted perfectly to a world dominated by humans. They are better suited to our habits even than our pets, the animals we have invited into our homes. It wasn't by accident. Rats are specially equipped with extraordinary powers.

Nocturnal by nature (although they will switch to days if they're living with a human who prefers nights), they have poor eyesight. They can barely see beyond four feet—although they can visually detect motion well up to about 50 feet—and are very close to color blind. To compensate, their other senses have developed to a remarkable degree.

They can detect and differentiate smells as well as the best of dogs. In fact, recent research has indicated that more than 1 percent of the rat's entire genetic structure is devoted to their sense of smell. Their hearing is acute—they can detect about two and a half times as many sounds as humans can—and specialized in location. If a rat is in your living room and you roll over in bed upstairs, it not only knows that you did it, but where you were when it happened. It's in a rat's best interest to be able to locate any potential threats and its ears can let it know where sounds originate. Because of the shape and the varying thicknesses of their earlobes, rats can swivel their ears and, by measuring and comparing differences in intensity, triangulate and accurately estimate the site of a sound's origin.

Even more keen is the rat's sense of taste. Laboratory tests have shown that rats can detect different tastes as small as 0.5 parts per million—about the equivalent of two grains of salt in a pound of peanut butter. That ability has constantly frustrated would-be poisoners, who must use greater amounts of increasingly stronger poisons as rats develop immunities, but have to keep them flavorless enough to prevent them from tipping off and scaring away their sensitive quarry. When a rat senses that something isn't quite right with a potential food source, it will urinate on it. This most likely serves as a warning to other rats, but I like to think it's also an editorial comment to less skilled rat hunters.

The most developed sense rats have, however, is touch. Using the whiskers on its face and other guide hairs over the length of its body, a rat can constantly feel its surroundings.

Rats depend on this sense so much that many actually feel uncomfortable if they can't feel a stationary object, like a wall, against at least one side. Only the most confident rats walk about in the open. This habit of sticking close to inanimate objects—called thigmophilia or "love of touching"—means that rats will often take familiar, security-inducing routes along walls. One Toronto health inspector told me that the first thing he does when he enters a restaurant kitchen is check the bases of the walls for grease trails left by rats leaning against them as they make their nightly rounds.

Complementing all those senses is the body of a superathlete. A rat can run, jump, and climb just as acrobatically as any tree squirrel. They can't sprint for very long, but their uncanny change-of-direction skills can usually frustrate even the most ardent pursuer. Rats can leap four feet straight up from a standing position. They can climb up vertical brick walls or a lead pipe. But, lacking rotating joints in their back legs, rats can't descend as quickly as their arboreal cousins. Rats compensate with an ability to bend in midair with a cat-like feetfirst fall. It's been frequently written that a rat can survive a 50-foot fall without injury, but truly reliable sources are hard to find. I have seen desperate rats survive falls from at least 30 feet without a shudder, though, so the 50-foot benchmark doesn't seem like an exaggeration. One night at about 3 a.m., I was walking my dog on West 109th Street between Amsterdam and Columbus avenues in Manhattan. Despite the hour, there was still a lot of pedestrian traffic and light. As I stopped to let Buckley sniff a garbage can, I heard a shuffle. I turned my head, and saw a medium-sized rat leap straight up through a layer of trash and well over my head. He landed on the rim of the can, jumped into the street away from my cowering dog and in between a speeding Volkswagen Passat and the Pontiac Grand Prix that was no more than five feet behind it. On the other side, the rat ran straight up a chain-link fence and into the Con Ed station.

Rats, which originally inhabited tropical swamps and riverbanks, are also excellent swimmers. And they still prefer to be close to water, often living in ports, waterfront parks and, of course, sewers. Wild rats can swim well enough to catch fish, and the stories about rats crawling up pipes and out of toilets are not entirely the stuff of urban legends. "I've seen rats in toilets a couple of times," said Marko, a superintendent at a high-rise in Vancouver. "At first I thought they went in there to escape, but I realized after a while that if they can get out that way, they must be getting in that way too." It's not a problem for a rat to crawl up a pipe, even if it's full of water or sewage, for as long as it can hold its breath (if necessary, up to three minutes). It can accomplish this feat even in smooth-bore pipes using a technique experts call "Santa Clausing"—pressing its back on one side of the pipe and its feet on the other and inching its way up. Many newer buildings use wider pipes, up to six inches in diameter, in an effort to prevent surprise visitors from emerging out of the toilet, but the exterminators I've spoken with say it won't do much good. A determined rat, they say, can always find a way in.

The normal way in for rats is the traditional hole in the wall. Although rats prefer a hole of about three inches in diameter (approximately the size of the mouth of a coffee mug), they can squeeze through holes no bigger than three-quarters of an inch wide when necessary. It may seem hard to believe that an animal the size of a man's shoe can fit through a hole the size of a quarter, but it can. One of the rat's most remarkable features is an ability to collapse its rib cage. Without a rigid set of ribs in the way, a rat can wriggle through any opening large enough for its head to fit through. That flexible skeleton also helps it absorb the impact of falls and blows from humans and other would-be assailants.

Of course, those blows are rare. Self-preservation appears to be the only concept more sacred to rats than eating and having sex, and they are well equipped to escape most assaults. Rats prefer to stay out of sight and, when spotted, flee almost immediately. At least, they almost always do. When I lived in New York, I would occasionally notice a few rats, no more than an arm's length away, confidently chewing on old bagels or hot dogs, seeming not to care about me or the other humans around them. Since then, I've seen the same phenomenon in other large, busy cities, like Paris. Although it's been postulated that intense competition in such places has created a super-rat with no fear of humans, I don't believe it. If a human pays even the slightest attention to these city rats, they quickly move on. They haven't lost their fear of humans; they've just learned that passing humans don't pose much of a threat. Who's going to take the time to kill a rat on the way to work? "I like to think of street rats as being like really bad transvestites," said Ben, a Brooklyn-based exterminator. "You put 'em someplace like Iowa or your living room and everyone's going to make a big fuss, but here in New York, people just keep on walking . . . they've got too much to do."

But if a rat can't blend into the background or escape, it will fight—and it is well equipped to do so. Each of those springy legs has a surprisingly strong paw with four claw-like nails, easily capable of opening human skin and usually teeming with dangerous bacteria.

But the rat's real weapon is its bite. Like all rodents, the rat has oversized incisors, which it uses to gnaw. It gnaws when it eats, it gnaws to make its home, it gnaws to get into your home, it gnaws when it's frustrated and it gnaws for fun. All that gnawing works like a grinding wheel on a rat's teeth, keeping them sharp and strong. You'll rarely see a rat with a broken tooth, as the hardness of the enamel on the front of a rat's incisors is comparable to some grades of steel. There is no enamel on the back of these teeth, which causes them to wear down more quickly than the front sides, ensuring a constantly sharp chisel-like shape. According to experiments conducted by Bell Labs, a rat can exert a force of 7000 psi (pounds per square inch) in a bite, much greater than the 1000 or so for a dog and 150 for most humans, although over a much smaller area. Teeth that can easily chew through a copper pipe or concrete glide through clothes and human flesh as though they were made of warm ice cream.

Rats have three types of bites, depending on why they are biting. They have an ordinary bite they use for feeding, but when they are chewing on something they don't want to eat, like wood, brick, or lead, a membrane slides down between the incisors to prevent the rat from swallowing any debris. They also have an aggressive bite they use when fighting, defending themselves, or killing prey. On those occasions, the rat's incisors separate to create a wider wound and more internal damage to its enemy. According to Jack Black, the Victorian-era impresario who described himself as the queen's rat catcher: "When a rat's bite touches the bone, it makes you faint in a minute, and it bleeds dreadful—ah, most terrible—just as if you had been stuck with a knife. You couldn't believe the quantity of blood that come away." He also described a rat bite that went through his thumbnail and another that made his "arm swole, and went as heavy as a ton weight pretty well, so that I couldn't even lift it, and so painful I couldn't bear my wife to ferment it. I was kept in bed for two months through that... I was so weak I couldn't stand, and I was dreadful feverish—all warmth like. I knew I was going to die, 'cause I remember the doctor coming and opening my eyes, to see if I was still alive."

As bad as a rat's bite can be, it's made much worse by their saliva. The fifty thousand or so people who report rat bites every year must also contend with the thought that they were also potentially exposed to hanta virus, typhus, the aptly named rat-bite fever, rat pox, salmonella, leptospirosis, eosiniphilic meningitis, and, in very rare cases, rabies. According to a 1995 study, 10 to 100 percent of pet rats and 50 to 100 percent of the wild rats in any given population in North America carry the rat-bite fever virus. It's fatal in 13 percent of cases in humans, despite antibiotic treatment.

Of course, a rat's bite hardly compares to a lion's. Lions actually eat people. But it happens so rarely that it generally makes worldwide news. In the fall of 2005, a pride of lions killed and ate twenty Ethiopian villagers and wounded ten others. Intensive farming in the area and the aftereffects of Ethiopia's war with Eritrea had stripped the area of any suitable prey species, so the remaining, starving lions had little choice but to eat some people. Within days, the Ethiopian army had killed them all. Of course, rats don't eat people—live ones, at least. While wild lions—usually driven to prey on humans only due to a lack of appropriate quarry or by injury or frailty—have been responsible for perhaps a few thousand or so humans deaths in recorded history, rats have killed in the hundreds of millions and continue to do so.

Rats starve us. Not only do they have an annoying habit of eating our food—from infesting grain silos to preying on poultry—but they also tend to leave their hairs, urine, and feces behind. Estimates by reliable sources (such as the World Health Organization) of the amount of the world's human food eaten or contaminated by rodents (mainly rats) range from 20 percent to 35 percent. David Pimental, an agriculture expert from Cornell University estimated that rats cause about $19 billion damage in food lost or spoiled every year in the U.S. alone. Rats are so prevalent that governments in many countries must put acceptable limits on how much rat contamination they deem to be safe. For example, the U.S. Food and Drug Administration allows "an average of two rodent hairs per one hundred grams of peanut butter," that's about nine per pound. Particularly hard hit by rats are developing countries where an infrastructure that can provide food security often doesn't exist. Rat infestations can severely worsen or even cause widespread famines.

Rats have also developed a taste for other human recipes, particularly for the insulation on electrical cables. Estimates by insurers and fire-safety groups put the proportion of non-intentional fires caused by rats as high as 25 percent.

It doesn't matter how much food you have if you have, however, the plague. Rats spread the plague, a condition synonymous with lethal pandemics. Purists will point out that rats don't actually give humans the plague, that it's really fleas that transmit the disease. But, throughout history, the fleas that carry the plague have almost invariably jumped from rats to humans. In fact, not all fleas carry the plague. Those that do prefer rats. In fact, they are so partial to rats that they will bite a different animal only under extreme duress. Plague, of course, is virtually always fatal in rats, and dead rats are no good to fleas. Faced with the prospect of starvation, rat fleas turn to the next best thing—usually humans.

Since the first recorded plague (the Old Testament describes how the Philistines were visited by the disease as a punishment for stealing the Ark of the Covenant), stories of its outbreaks are eerily repetitive. The disease arrived, people began to notice swelling of the lymph nodes in their armpits and groins, which later turned into sore, black pustules. Their skin would blacken as they began to bleed internally, then they died in great numbers. Affected areas could expect to see anywhere from 30 to 50 percent of their entire population die in days. Entire cities were erased from the map.

The ancient Greeks were hit by plague, as were the Romans and their contemporaries in North African civilizations. In the mid 14th century, the plague swept through Europe and much of Asia. The devastation was so bad that many in the affected areas considered it the end of the world. Streets were clogged with cholera-infected corpses, people made plans no longer than a few weeks in advance, all philosophy and religion were questioned and the world changed. About one-third of the residents of what was then referred to as "the civilized world" perished. Unable to think of anything more frightening, they called the plague the "Black Death."

They had no idea where it came from and not the slightest ability to do anything about it. All they could do was count the dead and pray for it to go away. Plague appeared in smaller, less lethal doses every few years after that. The last massive plague in Europe occurred in the 17th century. Better sanitation and a stricter, less tolerant attitude towards rats are generally given credit for the turnaround.

The last major pandemic occurred in Asia in the middle of the 19th century, killing twelve million people in China and India alone. Within a few decades, modern scientific method managed to isolate the virus, the flea, and the rat.

But don't think that the Black Death is extinct. The World Health Organization reports between 1000 and 3000 new cases every year. Particularly prevalent in Southwest Asia in countries around Kazakhstan, bubonic, pneumonic, and septicemic plague appears with frightening regularity in China, India, sub-Saharan Africa, South America, and the western and southwestern United States. In fact, fleas carrying bubonic plague were found on the carcasses of dead squirrels in public parks in Denver and Boulder, Colorado, in October 2005.

Although modern antibiotic treatment has brought the mortality rate below 15 percent and the disease is now mainly transmitted through wild rodents like the hoary marmot and black-tailed prairie dog, it's still quite possible that an encounter with a rat, even in the most developed of nations, can result in an infection with the disease—the bubonic plague!—and death.

As rats have been responsible for the deaths of hundreds of millions of humans over the years, humans have worked very hard to repay them. Mention is made of how annoying rodents can be—with threats most likely aimed at rats—in the Rig Veda, which dates to around 2500 BC and is considered the oldest preserved document in the world. The Romans, who held much of their wealth in stored grain, started spraying poisonous oils around farms and store-houses in an attempt to control rats in 200 BC and built their first "rat-proof" granary in 13 BC. Since then, humans have trapped, beaten, shocked, impaled, burned, and poisoned rats to death in immense numbers. Virtually every time a human has come into contact with a non-pet rat, he or she has done something to try to cause its death. And they have succeeded in great numbers. Pest control has become one of humankind's most steady and lucrative industries. People exterminate hundreds of millions of rats every year. In many parts of Africa and Asia, on the other hand, they're considered wild livestock and are eaten in large quantities. But their population continues to grow at a rate and to a size rivaled only among vertebrates by our own.

Of course, not every human believes the only good rat is a dead rat. Scientists have used rats for countless lifesaving experiments because the internal organs, brain structure, and social order of rats are uncannily like our own. And for a little more than a century, the habit of keeping rats as pets has grown and faded periodically. Their supporters consider them kind, clean, intelligent, and affectionate. Rats are part of our culture too. From the stories of ancient Indian deities to the Chinese zodiac to the gothic horror films of Hollywood, rats have been portrayed as villains, vermin, merry clowns, or faithful friends, but never seem to show up in the role of hero.

While virtually every other non-domesticated animal is rapidly vanishing, rats are enjoying a distribution and population far exceeding that which they would have had without human interference. They are in our forests, our parks, our walls, and our garages. They live in our homes, our stores, our factories, our hospitals, and our schools. They swim through our sewers and they hunt on our farms. They can be a cherished family pet, a lifesaving laboratory animal, or a snack served on a stick. Rats are everywhere humans are and even places we've left behind as too inhospitable.

As the other wild species on our planet—no matter how handsome, powerful, or regal they may be—are struggling to stave off extinction, the rat is enjoying remarkable success. While they bite us, destroy our infrastructure, steal millions of tons of our food and ruin even more, cause fires and spread deadly pandemics, there's little we can do about it. They horrify us and we fight back with traps, poisons, gasses, and mercenaries from the animal world like dogs, cats, and mongooses, but we make hardly a dent in their numbers. Rats are so good at adapting, surviving, and reproducing that there is little humankind can do but work on better rat traps and more potent poisons, and hope that the next plague they bring will be easy to recognize and stop.

Actually, there is one other animal that approaches the rat's success—the mouse. A sort of mini-rat with many of the same skills and habits, the mouse often lives in even closer contact with humans. "A mouse is stupid compared to a rat," said Ben the exterminator. "Mice take more chances and, consequently, get killed more often." But as a mouse is a smaller and far less complex animal than a rat, it's also far less capable of competing with us. Although the mouse has a population and distribution almost rivaling the rat's, it doesn't impact the lives of humans on nearly the same level. Very few humans hate or fear mice, they are relatively sim-ple to get rid of, and, despite their huge numbers, do a tiny fraction of the damage that rats do. And when rats and mice meet, the odds do not favor mice. "I tell people all the time they should be happy they have mice," said Ben. "If they have mice, that means they don't have rats—rats eat any mice they come across."

The rat may be small and ugly. It may not inspire awe as it nibbles and gnaws and skulks its way through life. But it can do something remarkable. It can compete with us as a wild animal and win. It hasn't become our friend like the dog or our captive like cattle, but instead lives alongside us, as constant companion, irritant, and sworn enemy. While human mistakes and negligence have led many species to extinction and thousands to the brink of annihilation, gargantuan, concerted efforts to rid ourselves of rats have failed miserably. There are more now than ever before and their population continues to boom. Truly it is the animal we can't get rid of, the only one capable of challenging human hegemony of the planet that deserves to be called King of Beasts.

"Don't Take Are Rats"

Sample from the online petition to stop the proposed ban of pet rats by the Saskatchewan government:

well i think its dum why band pet rats they are a great pet to have i enjoy haveing my pet rat studio with me all the time and the way i see it is if a dog or cat can have a good home to live in then a pet rat can too then if your going to band pet rats then you should band all anamals a rat is still a anamal and god put these anamls here for a reason and he is the one that put pet rats here so why dont you talk to god about it and why cant you guys just leave use alone and leave the anamals alone and stop sticking your noses were it doesnt belong this is canada its a free country we should be aload to have any anamal we want we all like diffrent types of anamals thats what makes use diffrent in my case i love pet rats maybe we should band the goverment and see how they like maybe then then they might know how rats and other anamals feel being denid and not wanted. well thats all i have to say and i hope it makes a diffrents

Source: petitiononline.com

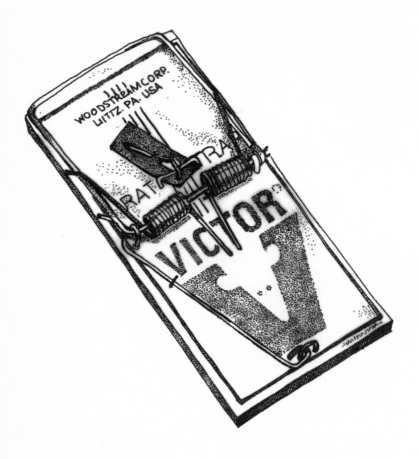

The Prehistory
of the Rat

O n the muddy banks of the slow-moving river we
English-speakers call the Mekong, a hunting civet
spotted a potential meal. The intended quarry was a
rodent, which gave the civet a surge of adrenaline. Rodents,
generally slow-moving and without much fight, are considered easy prey by many predators. This one was a bit
different, though. It had a naked tail, suggesting it swam;
but it also had a narrow, conical head, which indicated that
it was a burrowing animal. Stranger still was what it was
doing. From experience, the civet knew that rodents were
usually content just to gnaw on vegetables or nibble on
grain, but this one appeared to be eating the remains of a
rather large, freshly killed catfish. The civet realized that if it
planned right, it could get two meals out of one attack.
Stealthily, the civet crept behind the rodent and positioned
itself for attack. When it was confident that the ravenous

rodent was fully engrossed in its meal, the civet struck. Normally, the weight of a pouncing civet can break the back of a rodent, but this one had some fight in it. So much, in fact, that it managed to sink its incisors into the civet's right front paw, giving it a moment to slip away. While the stunned civet rolled over in searing pain, the large rodent sprung from the bank into the river and, with a flick of its long, hairless tail, swam away.

Such encounters were probably commonplace for early rats. Before they attached themselves to humans maybe ten thousand years ago, the rat was just another small animal trying hard not to be eaten. Perhaps a little better equipped than some of its competitors, with its powerful jaws and excellent leaping ability, the rat was already a success long before humans stood upright.

But the rat's story is not a clear one. Sadly, biologists are like everybody else, and the best and brightest are usually attracted to the most glamorous pursuits. While there may be plenty of texts devoted to lions, chimpanzees, and great white sharks, very little serious scientific research has been done in the field of rats. What we do know is that the family began sixty-five million years ago as the time of dinosaurs was just coming to an end. New and diverse types of mammals emerged to take the ecological niches formerly inhabited by dinosaurs. One group, the anagalids, was made up of small, scurrying critters with pronounced incisors. Typical of them was zalambdales, a pointy-nosed little insect eater with a long naked tail. About 8 inches long, if zalambdales were encountered today, it would probably be identified as a small rat, although its longer legs and shrew-like snout would make it a pretty funny-looking rat.

As zalambdales and other anagalids died out, the family split into two directions—the lagomorphs (rabbits and pikas) and the rodents. Identified by their lack of canine teeth and constantly growing incisors, opportunistic rodents flourished almost as soon as they appeared. About forty million years ago, a group of animals called the Ischyromyoidae, which looked and acted very much like modern-day ground squirrels, aside from a pair of horns on their snouts, probably represented the first real rodents. From them developed antemus (Latin for "before the mouse") sometime around fifteen million years ago. Forefather of the Murinidae family that includes many rats and mice that emerged in the Old World, antemus scurried around what is now Pakistan and Afghanistan and looked and behaved very much like modern mice and rats. About 3.5 million years ago, karnimata (the ancestor of the modern rat) appeared in Southeast Asia.

Since then, Murinidae has evolved to, by most reckonings, 519 separate species. With members like the stink mouse, Rummler's mosaic-tailed rat, the large-toothed giant rat, and the pencil-tailed tree mouse, Murinidae had established itself in Asia, Africa, Europe, and Australia and in every conceivable habitat long before humans arrived. Of course, there are lots of rodents we call "rats"—ranging from cute hopping kangaroo rats of the Southwest United States to the bizarre, blind, naked mole-rats of Africa, which exhibit decidedly insect-like behavior—but when we're talking about rats without any descriptive adjectives, we are talking about what scientists call rattus and we just call rat. Through a process called anagenesis—when the frequency of common mutations becomes so high that the original species is eventually entirely replaced by a new species—karnimata became rattus.

Rattus looked and acted much like today's rats, but without the benefit of living with humans. Prowling on the edges of the marshes, swamps, and riverbanks of the steamy jungles of Southeast Asia, rattus developed its remarkable skills and athleticism. Always the opportunist, rattus diverged from most other rodents by expanding its diet to include meat. A true omnivore, rattus not only ate carrion and insects, but also foraged for birds' eggs and young, caught fish, and hunted other small animals when they were available.

Maybe it was the protein or maybe it was the ability to find food under any circumstances, but rattus succeeded like few other creatures. It didn't come easily. The forests and swamps of Southeast Asia were an exceedingly tough neighborhood for small animals. Not only did rats have to deal with civets, tigers, leopards, other cats, wild dogs, owls, hawks, eagles, cobras, pythons, monitor lizards, and other predators on land and from the sky, but they also had to contend with crocodiles and big fish in the water.

Despite the dangers and competition, rattus succeeded so well that its biggest threat was overpopulation. Ever resourceful, rattus migrated and adapted to conquer new environments, diets, and habits. In parts of Indonesia and Northern Australia, rats became as specialized as the finches on the Galápagos Islands that inspired Charles Darwin to theorize about natural selection. Some of them hunt for fallen fruits and baby birds on the forest floor, while others climb trees for hanging fruits and arboreal insects. Hoogerwerf's rat, for example, is believed to live only on the riverbanks of one forest park on the Indonesian island of Sumatra. It shares this home with Korinch's rat (also first observed during the era when biologists enjoyed naming species after themselves and their colleagues), which looks virtually identical, but has a different diet and nesting behavior. Although their ranges overlap, the two rats rarely run into each other and live in relative harmony.

Other rats, perhaps carried by storms, arrived on smaller islands and adapted to their often unique habitats. The Timor rat thrives only in the misty teak forests of Timor, while others are endemic to their own islands, like the Mindoro climbing rat or the Tawitawi rat. That specialization may have helped rattus colonize new territory in prehistoric times, but it puts some species at risk now. About 100 miles northwest of where wild Sumatra and crowded Java meet, lies Enggano, a small island of rolling hills, swaying palms, and grassy meadows surrounded by jagged cliffs and unpredictable currents. Uninhabited by humans for centuries, the colonial Dutch used it as an unsupervised penal colony. The prisoners were said to have fed on rats. The human evolutionary experiment ended on the morning of August 27, 1883, when Krakatoa erupted, hurling 20 cubic kilometers of mostly molten rock into the sky. The ensuing tsunami wiped out the human population on Enggano, but the native rats survived. Since then the island has been slowly and cautiously repopulated, mainly by men who brave the dangerous waters in search of sea cucumbers, a bottom-dwelling invertebrate popular in Japanese cuisine, and the men and women who support the trade. Although their numbers are small, the most recent human invasion has played havoc on the rats' population, destroying their habitat and bringing along more aggressive descendants of the rattus clan. Powerful earthquakes and tsunamis in 2000 and 2005 again battered the island, killing a great deal of the human population and both

times destroying more than 90 percent of the island's buildings. While the humans are largely gone from the island,
their effects linger, as the rats they brought with them proved
more aggressive at finding food and nesting sites, the native
rats (as well as other local species) suffered. The Enggano rat
is now considered one of the most critically endangered
mammals in the world.

Some rats went farther away. One group went west to the
Indian subcontinent. They got larger and darker, and grew
longer tails to adapt to a life climbing undetected through the
dense foliage. Their long, naked tails not only helped them
balance on slender branches, they also served as thermoregula-
tors, sloughing off excess body heat in hot weather, like a dog's
tongue. For these rats, being off the ground meant security.
When they are frightened, their means of escape is virtually
always up—a tree, a cliff, a wall, a pipe, a wire, anything vertical
will do. Known to science as *Rattus rattus* but to everyone else
by names like black rat, tree rat, roof rat, house rat, and ship rat,
Rattus rattus lost much of its comfort in the water but gained
other skills and traits that insured its success. Black rats gained
the ability to reproduce quicker and in greater numbers than
any of its ancestors or contemporaries. And, to combat the rig-
ors of overcrowding, the black rat learned to live in groups.

There's little complex about a black-rat colony. Small
groups, generally related by no more than a couple of generations, band together for support, food sharing, and living
space with a limited level of mutual tolerance. Disputes are
solved with displays of aggression, the larger and stronger
rats invariably holding sway. Older and infirm rats are often
driven away, sometimes violently, with severe bites to the tail
and hindquarters.

While the black rat was emerging in India, more of rattus's descendants migrated north to become a very different kind of rat. Adapting to a number of cooler, often treeless environments as far north as Siberia, these rats grew larger, stronger, and furrier.

Rattus norvegicus, better known as the brown rat, Norway rat, sewer rat, wharf rat, or common rat, is just slightly longer than a black rat but generally about twice the weight. More people may know the *Rattus norvegicus* more familiarly as the Norway rat rather than the brown rat, but it's a total misnomer. Not only did brown rats not originate in Scandinavia, but Norway was one of the last countries they showed up in—they weren't recorded there until 1768. While it is true that many brown rats are not actually brown—I've seen white, creamy, gray, tawny, black, and colors that can only be described as looking like blondes and redheads—most of them are, and very few of them come from Norway. Further complicating things is that so-called black rats are just as often brown. Common rats aren't always the most

Worst of the Worst

Estimated annual cost of economic damage by various introduced species in the United States

Rats	$19,000,000,000
Cats	$6,000,000,000
Zebra mussels	$3,000,000,000
Birds	$2,100,000,000
Asiatic clam	$1,000,000,000
Fishes	$1,000,000,000
Pigs	$200,000,000
Dogs	$136,000,000
Mongoose	$50,000,000
Green crab	$44,000,000
Gypsy moth	$22,000,000
Fire ants	$10,000,000
Horses and burros	$5,000,000
Reptiles and amphibians	$604,000

Source: David Pimentel, Lori Lach, Rodolfo Zuniga, and Doug Morrison, College of Agriculture and Life Sciences, Cornell University

common. Most rats that live in houses aren't house rats. And wharf rats, sewer rats, ship rats, and roof rats live in a variety of different habitats. So while neither black rat nor brown rat is a perfect name, they do appear to be the best available.

While an adept, if ungainly, climber, the brown rat prefers to stay on the ground, especially near water and where tall vegetation provides cover from flying predators. Brown rats take advantage of their terrestrial environment by making what experts call runs—beaten-down trails about the width of an adult rat. These runs are thoroughfares that allow rats to travel at great speeds to places of interest, like food sources and burrow entrances. The rats become so used to and so confident in their runs that they rarely look where they're going. Scientists, perhaps with cruel senses of humor, have placed prominent barriers in runs and the rats have invariably conked their heads as they run into the objects at top speed.

Rats also communicate through sound. Beyond the squeaks, chirps, and shrieks humans can hear, rats have a range of vocalizations too high-pitched for humans to detect. While most of these "ultrasonic" vocalizations carry messages about mating, rats also use them to warn each other of predators and some rats have developed even bigger vocabularies. Those that live close to humans appear to have learned that it's not in their best interest to be heard, no matter how dire the message. So urban rats use ultrasonic communication much more frequently than rural rats and for less pressing matters.

Unlike the black rat, which prefers to build large spherical nests out of twigs and leaves in the lower branches of large trees and live on the ground only out of necessity, the brown rat generally lives underground, but occasionally in dead trees or caves. I've seen wild brown rats scurry about almost unseen among the decorative rocks in Manhattan's Inwood Park. While unsuspecting families throw pieces of bread to the ducks, geese, and even the fish in the Harlem River, a crew of rats—which would probably cause a panic if they were noticed—makes sure that none of the dropped or discarded pieces are wasted.

Although they generally dig their own burrows, brown rats are not reluctant to take over an existing burrow, often after eating the previous occupants. Brown rats line the birth chambers and nurseries of their burrows and store grain and other foods in separate rooms. Fermentation of plant material, mixed with ammonia from the rats' urine, can also, under the right circumstances, produce enough heat to keep the entire burrow complex warm in winter.

While much of the wild brown rat's natural diet is made up of plants, it appears to prefer meat when it can get it and has been observed taking down prey as large as young pigs. Recent studies have shown that a rat's dietary needs are similar to a human's, although rats generally need to consume a much higher proportion of their body weight in food each day.

An inability to vomit has led to rats being very suspicious of new foods. When presented with an unfamiliar food, a rat will almost always ignore it. Instead, it prefers to eat what's it's used to—even if it's much less nutritious. But if familiar food is lacking or a bold rat is feeling adventurous, it will take a few small nibbles at the new food and wait for its body to react. Rats, like humans, can connect ill feeling to the food that precipitated it, even if the cause and effect are hours away. Should there be no ill effects, the rat will deem the new food edible.

This caution, coupled with a need for a varied diet, leads to what scientists call the omnivore's paradox—rats (and other omnivores like pigs, bears, and humans) need a variety of foods to stay healthy, but also need to avoid dangerous, potentially lethal items that may appear to be food. The result is that omnivorous animals tend to have highly developed senses and great memories. They are also generally social. By watching the behavior of other, more experienced rats, young members of the colony can learn which foods are safe and which aren't. If a healthy rat returns to the burrow smelling of potatoes, other rats will recognize potatoes as a potentially safe food source. Should a rat smelling of carrots appear unwell, its peers will avoid carrots. Also like humans, rats develop appetites influenced by what its body is lacking. A rat in need of protein will seek out meat, and one needing vitamins will search for fruit.

Similarly, rats have developed a trait humans call neophobia—the fear of the new. When a new object is placed in a rat's environment, it will do all it can to avoid it. Because of this, professional exterminators will often leave baited, but unset, snap traps in a rat-infested house for days. It's only once the rats get used to the traps as a benign part of their environment that they can be set.

Among new scents, sights, and sounds, brown rats have developed an uncanny ability to discern predators. Experiments have shown that captive brown rats that have not been exposed to cats for two hundred generations will flee at the scent of a cat and stay hidden until the scent dissipates. At such times, rats survive on stored food until they are sure the danger has passed. When smells of animals that present little if any danger to the rats—cows, for example—

are introduced, they become curious, perhaps a little cautious, but hardly panicked.

Ironically, rats also have an instinct for neophilia—love of the new. B. F. Skinner, an American scientist generally lauded as the greatest behaviorist of his time, conducted all kinds of experiments with rats that increased humankind's knowledge of the rat's brain and their own. Of Skinner's findings, perhaps the most surprising was that, although rats fear new items in a familiar territory, they are also fascinated by new territory. When Skinner put a rat into an unfamiliar box, he noticed the first thing it would do was explore. Taking the experiment to its furthest degree, Skinner placed starving rats in unfamiliar boxes with food. Rather than voraciously devour the food (as the scientists had expected), the rats explored every square inch of their new home, then ate the food. Further experiments added credence to the idea that lonely rats will look for other rats even if it means they must endure hardship or risk their lives in the search. Clearly, rats appreciate the company of other rats, especially when they're old enough to mate.

Falling somewhere in between the chaos of a black-rat clan and the fiercely enforced hierarchy of a wolf pack, brown-rat colonies are easygoing family groups with complex but variable organization. Members generally tolerate one another and can be affectionate (although a hungry rat may engage in cannibalism when the opportunity arises) and will even feed infirm or otherwise disabled members. Brown rats often make friends with other members and can become depressed if they are separated. They can also make enemies and fight, usually using their paws as bludgeoning weapons, saving their potentially lethal bites for more threatening enemies or prey. These scuffles establish and maintain a pecking order that roughly corresponds to how much food a rat gets and how often it mates. Fights rarely go beyond a punch to the face or a body slam, but male rats looking for a better place in the community have been known to kill rats higher up in the pecking order than them. More often, young rats who were bested by adults will remain submissive even after they've outgrown their aggressors, appearing to prefer a harmonious colony to pursuing their own ambitions. They seem well aware that a battle can quickly escalate to lethal proportions and that surviving losers are often banished from the colony.

Rat colonies don't usually have a leader in the sense normally associated with other animal groups, but a large male will usually emerge as the rat that mates most often and gets the most food. The rat's long tail and habit of living in large, chaotic groups gave rise to a strange phenomenon which led medieval Europeans—certainly an imaginative group—to rationalize the existence of a rat king. Every so often, in the frenzy of feeding or mating, rats may get their tails knotted together. When this happens, the entwined rats are sometimes cared for by other members of the colony but are doomed to die unless they can become unentangled. Historically, circles of from three to thirty-two dead rats connected at the tail have been found. On most of these occasions, the people who found them satisfied their curiosity with the bizarre explanation that the rats' tails were tied together by other rats to form a sort of living throne for the rat king, whose regal paws they supposed were far too important to touch the ground. They'd probably be disappointed by the actual story and by the fact that the rats have no king.

Instead, the dominant male is more like the captain of a sports team—widely regarded as the best at what he does and given respect, but with little dictatorial power unless push really comes to shove. Even in those situations, the top rat works on an individual basis, not as a commander.

Through colonial living, brown rats developed a special olfactory apparatus called the vomeronasal organ (VNO). Inside the nasal cavity, the VNO allows the rat to decode pheromones, the chemical signals emitted by other rats. This ability almost gives brown rats another sense. Pheromones carry information about a rat's mating and courtship status, overall health, mood, and level of aggression. They can be found in a rat's urine, feces, and secretions from glands in their skin. Baby rats, sensing their mother's diet from the pheromones in her milk, will usually attempt to eat the same foods, instinctively knowing them to be safe. Rats will often leave messages to other rats by urinating on an object it claims as its own—a habit that can annoy pet-rat owners, especially when the item in question is the rat's favorite human.

The strongest of all pheromones are those produced by a female who is ready to mate. In places of sparse rat population, the scent can be detected as far as ten miles away and any male rats within the radius will follow it. In areas of denser population, the scent kicks off a frenzy. The female runs throughout the colony, spreading the scent as thoroughly as possible. Surprisingly, this causes very little fighting and bickering. Instead, males ordinarily line up almost politely for a chance to mate. The most dominant rat always goes first, followed by the second strongest and so on, until the female eventually tires and retreats. Since even the most subordinate males often get a chance to mate—unlike more strictly enforced hierarchies like wolves—the pecking order is rarely questioned. Since the female mates with so many males, the presence of an infertile partner is of little consequence. In the furious jumble of serial mating, at least one potent sperm will hit its mark.

The young, often called pups, are born blind, hairless, and tiny. Since they are so stunningly helpless, they require constant care from their mother (the males, perhaps understanding the vagueness of paternity, offer no help). Should she abandon the litter even briefly, the offspring are in grave danger. Not only are the defenseless infants sought after by the regular array of predators—baby rats are popularly sold in the pet industry as "pinkies" to the owners of snakes, piranhas, and other carnivorous animals because of their inability to defend themselves or injure their assailant—but other rats, particularly males, will also eat them. Since male rats only rarely eat the offspring of females they have mated with, the female's solicitation of multiple partners makes even more sense.

From finding food to reproducing, brown rats are generally better than black rats at everything other than climbing. Just how skilled brown rats are at surviving was starkly illustrated in 2005 when scientists from New Zealand caught an urban brown rat in Auckland with a live trap baited with chocolate. The scientists took Razza, as they named the rat, to Motuhoropapa, an isolated island with no resident land mammals. With the help of a radio collar, they tracked Razza's every movement. For the first few days, he explored every square inch of the treeless 23.5-acre island. The scientists assumed he was looking for other rats. When he found none, he established a smaller home range and fed on penguins, their eggs and their young. And, after four weeks, he wriggled out of his tracking collar and the scientists lost his trail. "If this had been a pregnant female rat it would have been a problem," said biologist Mick Clout of the University of Auckland's School of Biological Sciences. "It takes only one of them to establish a population."

With the experiment declared over, teams of scientists armed with snap traps, live traps, and glue traps combed the island. After ten weeks of frustration and empty traps, the scientists called in the dogs. They scoured the island and found nothing. It was only by chance that another scientist happened to see Razza on Otata, another, much smaller uninhabited island. Apparently, the rat had swum the rough, predator-infested 1300-foot saltwater gap between the islands because he was looking for a female rat to mate with. Once he was satisfied that there were no other rats on Motuhoropapa, he went looking for them on the closest piece of land. Eight more weeks of traps baited with chocolate, peanut butter, and bacon grease failed to catch Razza. "We were literally tearing our hair out at times trying to find this animal," Clout said. The dogs eventually cornered Razza on a small peninsula and he met his end on a snap trap baited with penguin meat.

"We didn't know it would be this difficult to trap one rat," said New Zealand Department of Conservation biologist David Towns. It was. One rat, taken from a big-city alley and brought to two small barren islands with no other land animals, managed to evade dozens of scientists, hundreds of traps, and a troop of dogs for almost half a year, despite the fact that they were the ones who'd put him there. The experiment had a resounding conclusion—brown rats are very good at staying alive.

Black rats aren't quite as hardy as their bigger cousins. Although black rats once thrived in places like Europe and the cooler reaches of North and South America, they are now restricted primarily to very warm climates. Where they have lived together, brown rats usually force black rats up out of their way and eventually out. Not only are brown rats stronger and more aggressive, they are not always reluctant to include black rats in their diet.

In spite of their weakness in the face of their bigger, stronger cousin, it was black rat's that first made the jump that guaranteed its continued existence on our planet. It was black rats who timidly approached human settlements in search of food, shelter, and protection from predators. It was black rats who invaded our homes and eventually grew to prefer them to their wild habitats. It was black rats who first ate our food, gnawed on our walls, and spread terrifying diseases. Nobody knows when rats took to our homes—a concept we call "commensalism"—but the fact that they did was their ticket to long-term biological success.

According to biologists, a commensal animal is one that lives with another animal but does not actually harm its host as a parasite does and doesn't help it as a symbiotic partner does. The term comes from the Latin *con mensa*, which means "to share a table." A typical commensal relationship would be the way remoras (sucker fish) attach themselves to sharks in hopes of scrounging a free meal after the shark kills its prey. Rats followed ancient humans around, eating the scraps from their kills and their harvests. As some humans learned that keeping prey species as domestic animals and planting specific crops made the prospects of a steady diet more certain, rats moved into our corrals and farms and eventually our houses.

The black rat had the good fortune to settle in areas of great commerce. Long before Marco Polo started his journey east in 1271, China and India were already centers of rich trading, with commercial interests as far away as the eastern Mediterranean. Black rats hitched along on caravans and sailing vessels—a mode of transport they are known to be well suited for, hence the name "ship rat"—and established viable populations throughout Asia. Trade with Europe was limited, and few rats made their way there until the Crusades. Beginning in 1063 and ending in 1291, the Crusades were a series of usually ill-conceived military campaigns by European Christians bent on ridding the Holy Land of Muslims. While the plan ultimately failed, the Crusaders brought back spices, silk, and rats. It was black rats who overran Europe in the medieval period and it was black rats who carried the fleas that brought the Black Death.

Although nobody at the time suspected that rats were the vector on which the Black Death traveled, they were not a welcome sight. Almost as long as humans have existed, they have been living with and trying to get rid of rats. Cleanliness wasn't a pressing issue with Europeans back then (most slept in the same buildings as their livestock), but the theft of food was. At a time when famine was never far from people's minds, the thought of an animal that ate food humans claimed as their own and did not provide meat, milk, eggs, or skins must have been infuriating. But, over the millennia, only one thing has proven able to rid an area of black rats—brown rats.

Brown rats came late to Europe, mainly because nobody there ever traded with the people who lived in the Mongolian, Manchurian, and Siberian plains brown rats started out in. But enterprising brown rats eventually made their way to Europe and North America simply by being successful enough to expand their range incrementally westward—tagging along on military campaigns helped too. The earliest mention of what were indisputably brown rats in Europe is a tale of hordes of them in 1727 desperately trying to find a way to cross the Volga River (traditionally considered the dividing line between Europe and Asia). Since brown rats were reported in England less than a year later, they probably arrived in the continent much earlier. One of the few truly great biologists of the medieval age, a Swiss genius named Conrad Gessner, drew what appears to be a brown rat in a volume of his masterwork, *Historiae animalium*, in 1553. Since Gessner called the entry "rattus," scientists over the centuries believed that he'd drawn a very robust black rat, common and widespread in Europe at the time, or that he wasn't all that much of an illustrator. But in his description of the "rat" species, Gessner refers to the occurrence of all-white rats. Since albinism almost never cropped up in black rats back then, he may actually have been studying and drawing brown rats. Whichever rat Gessner was describing, it didn't do him any favors. Despite having a medical doctorate as one of his many honors, Gessner died of the plague in December 1565.

The first scientist to write extensively about brown rats as a separate species was John Berkenhout, who published *Outlines of the Natural History of Great Britain and Ireland* in 1769. Given the honor of naming the species, he called it *Rattus norvegicus* (meaning Norway rat, a name many people still use, especially in Britain) because he first encountered them on ships carrying lumber from Norway. Modern scholars disagree on where Berkenhout went wrong, but he was definitely wrong, as "Norway rats" didn't even appear in

Norway until some years after they had become well established in Great Britain and had only just arrived there when
Berkenhout published. While many now believe that the
ships were actually from Denmark and Berkenhout confused
them with Norwegians because of their similar language,
others have said that he discovered the rats on ships arriving
from the Netherlands and that he blamed the Norwegians
because he was of Dutch origin and did not want to sully the
reputation his own nation.

At any rate, brown rats acquired a dominant position in
Europe and North America before very long. Black rats had
more than a hundred-year head start in North America
before browns arrived in 1755, and were considered commonplace by 1775.

The story is basically the same everywhere in temperate
areas. Established black rats usually have a time of coexis-
tence with invading brown rats, but their larger, more
aggressive cousins push them up into the trees before too
long. For many years in Europe, it was not uncommon for a
building to have brown rats living in the sewers and basement and black rats living in the attic or roof. The area in
between became a no-rat's land in which both species foraged as best they could. But eventually black rats were usually
pushed out altogether by the faster-breeding, more competitive browns. Although brown rats very rarely attack black rats
intentionally (unless one has invaded a brown-rat colony or
black rat young happen to be left unguarded), experiments
have shown that black rats can be intimidated by brown rats,
much as smaller rats defer to larger rats within their own
colony. That ill feeling can even make both sexes of rats
unwilling to breed. The mere presence of a few brown rats,

especially large ones, is usually enough to force black rats to seek higher ground.

While only a century ago, black rats ranged all over the United States and into Canada, competition with brown rats has limited them to just a few colonies in the palm trees above Los Angeles and a few other warm-weather cities. Although black rats are rarely spotted or trapped away from human settlement, scientists in the southwestern parts of the U.S. regularly find evidence of them in owl pellets, which suggests that a healthy wild population exists.

The overall population of rats in any area is a hard-to-determine statistic that's almost always inaccurately reported. Although the figure of one rat to one person is generally stated as the industry standard, figures as high as ten to one and even a thousand to one have been published, usually by politicians in an attempt to discredit a rival or increase a budget, or a newspaper trying to boost single-copy sales. The confusion started in 1909 with a combination of lazy research, some sloppy math, and sincere intentions. When W. R. Boelter was researching his book *The Rat Problem*, he toured rural areas of England, asking landowners if they had about one rat per acre. The vast majority agreed and those that didn't claimed they had more. People have always seemed to enjoy overstating the size and populations of rats they have to put up with. Boelter didn't bother asking people in towns or cities about their rat populations, assuming that densities in urban areas were just naturally higher than rural ones. Since Boelter, like all Englishmen at the time, knew there were 40 million acres in Britain, he postulated that there were forty million rats in the nation. By sheer happenstance, there happened to be forty million people in Britain at the time, so Boelter told the world that in places where people lived, there was a standard ratio of one rat per person. And everybody believed him.

That fallacy still persists, mainly because it's useful, despite the fact that it's been repeatedly proven untrue. David Davis, certainly the most acclaimed expert on the biology of urban rats, started his extensive and exhaustive study of rat populations in Baltimore in 1949. From there, he moved to New York City, working primarily in Harlem and other neighborhoods associated with high rat densities. He, and others after him, found that in urban areas, there is generally about one rat for every thirty-six human residents. While many claim and many more believe that there are about eight million or even eight billion rats living in New York City, a more accurate estimate—using Davis's 1:36 ratio and a human population of about eight million—would be closer to 250,000. Densities in non-urban areas, of course, vary greatly, depending mostly on food supply. Although grain, storage facilities and poultry farms can attract huge swarms of rats, Boelter was actually correct in his belief that cities and towns usually have higher rat population densities than rural areas.

But as one travels closer to the equator and the living gets easier, overall rat populations generally increase. And so does the percentage of black rats. In Calcutta, Rangoon, and Northern Australia, you'll not only find black rats and brown rats coexisting (on different levels, of course), but black rats in the majority. In the rest of the world, however, if brown rats are around, the black rats are probably gone.

Phantom Bites

While it is frequently published that people are much more likely to be bitten by other humans than rats, that assertion is at best misleading and probably altogether wrong. According to a number of medical studies, rats are responsible for more bite-related visits to hospitals than any species other than humans in the United States. But, human bites are virtually always inflicted by means of violent confrontation, often mutual, and police or other parties are usually involved. Rat bites, on the other hand, are frequently inflicted while the victim is asleep and, in the unlikely event he or she was aware of what happened, the victim is often too young to communicate it properly or simply isn't believed. Many other rat bites occur when the victim's hand has been placed in a dark hole or passageway. Since the rat is rarely seen and the entry wound may appear small, many bites are misidentified as an encounter with a nail or other sharp object.

Sources: Public Health Reports, Pediatrics, U.S. Public Health Service

A Most Uneasy Partnership

There's a woman who lives just outside Bakersfield, California, who has the best party anecdote in the world. The woman, let's call her Sophie, has survived the Black Death.

In the warm spring of 1995, she was piloting her rider mower on her huge backyard, not really paying attention to anything more than the warm California sun, when she heard an awful noise and felt a bump. When she got off the mower to go check what it was, she was saddened to find out that she had run over a ground squirrel—what the locals call a "gopher." She put the body in a plastic bag and placed it on the back of the mower until she could return to the house and toss it into the garbage.

She didn't think much of the incident—the deaths of small wild mammals rarely mean much to humans—and quickly forgot about it. So she was surprised when doctors in the emergency room asked her if she'd been in contact with any wild rodents. While it may not be well known to many of the people who live in the area, most doctors in western North America are aware that many of the most dangerous and mysterious diseases can be communicated by exposure to wild rodents.

The 57-year-old Sophie had gone to the hospital when her fever stabilized at 103, her diarrhea wouldn't stop, and she developed a strange, painful lump in her groin. She didn't believe the doctors when they told her she had contracted bubonic plague. Like most North Americans, Sophie thought that the plague was a medieval disease and had been controlled like polio or eradicated like smallpox.

She was wrong. In fact, according to the World Health Organization, there are between a thousand and three thousand new cases of bubonic plague reported every year. Even with proper medical attention, about one in every seven of those cases is fatal. And it doesn't just occur in what are often condescendingly called developing nations. The plague is rare, but present, in places like California, Utah, and British Columbia. Interestingly, plague is most often reported in southern Asia—where rats originated.

A number of rat advocates have asked me to make it clear that humans do not catch the bubonic plague from rats. They are right insomuch as guns don't kill people but bullets do. People don't get the plague from rats or their bites. They get it from fleas. In particular, they get it from one flea— *Xenopsylla cheopsis*, better known as the rat flea. The rat flea loves rats and will only bite another animal if there are no rats available. But rats are just as susceptible to plague as any other flea carrier. When a plague-affected flea bites a rat, it injects some of the plague—a rod-shaped bacterium known to scientists as *Yersinia pestis*—as it sucks its host's blood. When the rat dies of plague, the fleas hop off in search of another host. They'd prefer another rat but will make do with other animals if there are none around. *Xenopsylla cheopsis* became historically significant because its second favorite food just happens to be human blood.

The plague emerged in Western culture in the Old Testament. In the book of Samuel, God punished the Philistines of Ashdod with the plague for stealing the Ark of the Covenant from the children of Israel. Although English translations have often referred to the affliction the Philistines suffered as hemorrhoids, they were off by a few inches. The ancient texts actually speak of "a swelling in the secret parts"—one of the first symptoms of the plague is a massive, painful swelling of the lymph nodes in the groin. The swollen nodes, which also occur (usually later) in the underarms and on the throat, give the disease its name. When a person has the plague, the lymph nodes, small filters in the body's immune system, swell and bleed. This results in the formation of painful egg-sized lumps, blackened by blood, called buboes. Other symptoms include severe headaches, constant diarrhea, chills, fever, muscular pain, malaise and irritability. Significantly, the same sacred texts also mention that the Philistines were affected by a "ravaging of mice"—a fact made even more interesting when one considers that the ancient Israelites didn't have different words for mice and rats. Although no numbers are given, the texts do indicate that a large proportion of the Philistines' total population perished.

The plague appeared again in 430 BC during the Peloponnesian War, when it tore through North Africa and

Greece, wiping out a third of Athens, including the influential leader Pericles. The Greeks mention the plague striking
again in the first century AD when historian Rufus of
Ephesus recorded details of an outbreak in North Africa. He
wrote that Alexandra-based physicians Dioscorides and
Posidonius reported symptoms beginning with fever, pain,
agitation, and delirium. They described the buboes in
detail—large, hard, painful, and nonsuppurating (dry). Since
Rufus, perhaps showing some modesty, said they appeared
in "the usual places," it would appear that the Greeks were
pretty familiar with the disease.

Those epidemics were small compared to what happened to the eastern Roman Empire a century later.
Constantinople was the world's most influential city at the
time and much of its wealth lay in its massive granaries.
Every day, ships containing huge quantities of grain arrived
from all over the Mediterranean, especially the fertile Nile
Delta in Egypt. Rats carrying plague-affected fleas disem-
barked in Constantinople in 541 and invaded the city's grain
supply. Pretty soon, the disease spread to humans and the
effects were catastrophic. At the plague's worst, the citizens
of Constantinople were burying five thousand plague victims a day. Modern historians estimate that by the time the
disease wore itself out six months later, 40 percent of the
people in of the city and 25 percent of all of the humans in
the eastern Mediterranean had succumbed.

The world's first recorded pandemic led to another. In
588, grain—and rats and fleas—imported from the eastern
Mediterranean sparked an outbreak of the plague in what is
now France and spread in all directions. Little written material survives from that horrible time, but historians now

generally agree that many people, as many as twenty-five million, or about one-third of the total affected population, died.

The plague showed up in cycles of small epidemics for the next few centuries, each time devastating a city or region then passing away without human intervention. There was nothing people could do about the plague other than pray it wouldn't come to them and that it would go away if it arrived. It was just one of the many terrifying aspects of life in the Dark Ages until it became the most destructive force humanity had ever witnessed. It began, according to tradition, with an early attempt at biological warfare in one of the seemingly interminable conflicts between European and Asian powers.

In the early 1330s, the plague emerged in northern China and took an enormous number of lives (estimates vary as written records are scarce) before spreading westward. In 1346, it struck the Tatars in the Black Sea port city of Caffa (now known as Fedossia, Ukraine). The Muslim Tatars blamed the disease on the small community of Christian Genoese, who had established a thriving trading business in the city. When they realized that they were in danger, the Genoese quickly fortified their neighborhood, which the Tatars immediately put under siege. The Genoese held out until an innovative Tatar officer catapulted two plague-stricken corpses over the walls the defenders had managed to erect. The Genoese quickly contracted the disease and fled back to Italy. When rats carrying plague-afflicted fleas emerged from their ships on landing, the fate of Europe was sealed.

The plague took three forms in Europe, all of which can be traced back to the rat flea. The now-familiar bubonic plague was the most common form, with a mortality rate of between 30 and 75 percent of infections. It brought with it pneumonic plague, in which victims coughed up blood-engorged mucus and died very quickly. The pneumonic form of the disease had a mortality rate of around 95 percent, which prevented it from spreading very quickly, as the afflicted generally died before they could get very far. The third form of the plague was septicemic, in which the afflicted party suffered from disseminated intravascular coagulation. That means the victim's blood simply stops flowing. The mortality rate for this form approached 100 percent, with almost all of its victims dying the same day that symptoms appeared. Even today, there is no reliable or effective treatment for septicemic plague. As unoxygenated blood collected under the afflicted's skin, the body turned purple, almost black. This phenomenon may have given the plague its medieval name, the Black Death, as blackened corpses appeared in piles throughout Europe, although it can be argued that the Scandinavian chroniclers who first coined the phrase generally used the word "black" to describe anything they considered dreadful or terrifying. All three forms of the plague carried with them an astonishing stench, distributed through the sweat, phlegm, blood, urine or feces of the affected individual.

By December 1350, the plague had spread throughout the European continent, including Britain, Ireland, the inhabited areas of Scandinavia, and even Greenland. It followed traditional trade routes as flea-carrying rats stowed away aboard ships and caravans. As millions were dying, terrified people tried everything they could to fight a disease that none of them understood. Plague doctors took to wearing long pointed cones full of herbs on their faces—an early attempt at gas masks. The headgear gave doctors the appearance of giant, sinister birds, and offered little protection from the disease. Doctors are said to have died in staggering numbers as they administered useless potions, salves, and inhalations to their doomed patients. In his *Florentine Chronicle*, Marchione di Coppo Stefani reported:

> Neither physicians nor medicines were effective. Whether because these illnesses were previously unknown or because physicians had not previously studied them, there seemed to be no cure. There was such a fear that no one seemed to know what to do. When it took hold in a house it often happened that no one remained who had not died. And it was not just that men and women died, but even sentient animals died. Dogs, cats, chickens, oxen, donkeys and sheep showed the same symptoms and died of the same disease. And almost none, or very few, who showed these symptoms, were cured. The symptoms were the following: a bubo in the groin, where the thigh meets the trunk; or a small swelling under the armpit; sudden fever; spitting blood and saliva (and no one who spit blood survived it). It was such a frightful thing that when it got into a house, as was said, no one remained. Frightened people abandoned the house and fled to another.

People burned everything they could—especially fragrant herbs—to drive it away; they rang church bells and fired cannons constantly in an effort to scare it away with noise. As useless as those remedies were, there were worse. Authorities would frequently wall in houses suspected of containing plague, trapping the humans inside, but allowing the rats and fleas to escape. Some communities suspected dogs and cats of having something to do with the contagion and they were killed in massive numbers. Without these natural predators, rat populations exploded. And, just as the Muslims had blamed the Christians in their midst for the plague, so Christian Europeans accused the Jews among them of poisoning their wells despite the fact that Jews suffered as badly from the disease as anyone else. They were persecuted mercilessly, with entire communities of innocent people incinerated.

The mortality was enormous (about a third of Europe, or two hundred million people, perished). Not surprising that most people, as we have seen, assumed it was the end of the world. An English monk named John Clyn chronicled the effects of the plague in a monastery in Ireland until he too fell victim. He wrote:

> So that notable deeds should not perish with time, and be lost from the memory of future generations, I, seeing these many ills, and that the whole world encompassed by evil, waiting among the dead for death to come, have committed to writing what I have truly heard and examined; and so that the writing does not perish with the writer, or the work fail with the workman, I leave parchment for continuing the work, in case anyone should still be alive in the future and any son of Adam can escape this pestilence and continue the work thus begun.

At the bottom of Clyn's final page there is a note, written by another hand, which reads: "Here, it seems, the author died."

But the world didn't end and neither did the Black Death. The plague reappeared in smaller epidemics every dozen years or so. The best recorded of these outbreaks was the Great Plague of London that began in 1664. The disease had been around at a low level in the Netherlands since 1654 and is believed to have arrived in London from rats aboard Dutch cotton-trading ships. The disease first appeared among the workers in the suburban docks, but since the deaths of the poor were not habitually recorded, it's still unknown how many actually died. The very harsh winter of 1664–65 prevented the plague from spreading quickly, but when spring arrived, the disease headed into the great city. On April 12, 1665, Margaret Porteous became the first of about 110,000 plague deaths recorded that year.

As soon as it became clear that plague had struck the city, most of its inhabitants who had the means to leave London did. Bereft of most its nobility (King Charles II and his family relocated to Oxford), clergy, business class, doctors and apothecaries, the poor of London were left to die and fight the disease as best they could. During the summer, people were dying at a rate of about seven thousand a week. Again, people prayed, burned things, made noise, and persecuted Jews (who, as before, contracted the disease at roughly the same proportion as the rest of the population), but nobody suspected rats or their fleas. It seemed as though the plague would grow into another Black Death, but it soon came to an abrupt end.

On the night of September 2, 1665, a baker named Thomas Farrinor forgot to extinguish one of his ovens in his shop on Pudding Lane. Sparking embers from the oven ignited some nearby firewood and The Great Fire of London had begun. When first alerted to news of the fire, beleaguered London mayor Sir Thomas Bloodworth declared it so small that "a woman might piss it out." He was wrong. The fire raged for four days, ravaging the city's poorer districts and destroying 13,200 houses and 87 churches including St. Paul's Cathedral. Officially, only sixteen people died in the conflagration, but modern estimates put the total death toll among the poor at well over a hundred thousand.

The mayor reacted by banning highly combustible thatched roofs within the city, a law that survives today (the Globe Theatre, rebuilt in 1997, was the first thatched roof allowed in London since the fire, and its construction required special permission and many conditions). Without realizing it, however, the city had taken the first effective step against the plague in history. Thatched roofs are not only flammable, but they are ideal habitat for black rats. The rats sleep in burrows made in the thatching during the day, then sneak into the house to feed during the night. Even today, thatched roofs harbor immense numbers of black rats throughout communities in much of non-urban Africa.

Although the removal of thatching didn't wipe out rats in London, it certainly reduced their numbers and their proximity to humans. The burned-down parts of the city were rebuilt under the plans of architect Christopher Wren. His new vision for the city, which included widened streets and a modern sewage system, was implemented without compromise. As other sanitary measures improved in London and throughout Europe, the plague became less and less frequent, and outbreaks eventually ceased.

Although Europe was largely off the hook, the rest of the world wasn't. Bubonic plague occurred fairly regularly in small magnitudes in Central and Eastern Asia for centuries. A major outbreak in the northern Chinese province of

Yunnan in 1855 was effectively and brutally contained by military force as soldiers prevented anyone—infected or not—from leaving the area. The plan unraveled when a Muslim rebellion in the area sent thousands of plague-afflicted refugees south and east. Rats went with them. By 1894, at least twelve million people (and probably many more) had died. Rats aboard ships spread the pandemic to India in 1896, Africa in 1898, South America and the United States in 1899, and Russia in 1900.

A number of scientists came to the affected parts of Asia to find the source of the menace. One of them was a Swiss medical student named Alexandre Yersin, who had acquired French citizenship in order to study in Paris. A protégé of Louis Pasteur's, the two met after Yersin accidentally cut himself operating on a man who had been bitten by a feral dog. Yersin ran to the famed bacteriologist's office for treatment. He showed such a great natural talent for microbiology that Pasteur took him under his wing and eventually sent him to French Indochina (what's now Vietnam, Laos, and Cambodia) and Hong Kong to investigate the still-raging pneumonic plague.

Relatives of the deceased, Yersin would learn, were often reluctant to share the bodies of their loved ones and, despite the huge number of deaths, scientists in Hong Kong usually had a hard time acquiring samples. As the story goes, Yersin (who was fluent in English) befriended a Scottish priest who introduced him to a pair of Royal Navy morgue guards whom the impatient microbiologist promptly bribed. With samples hastily taken from the corpses of two British sailors who'd succumbed to the plague, Yersin rushed back to the hut he shared with distinguished Japanese microbiologist

Shibasaburo Kitasato outside the Pasteur Institute's Hong Kong office. After a number of exhaustive tests, Yersin experienced a eureka moment. After taking his eye off his microscope, Yersin wrote, perhaps with a shaking hand, "This is, without question, the microbe of the plague." He named the bacillus *Yersinia pestis*—Yersin's plague.

After some thought, Yersin remembered that some villagers in northern China reported that before the plague struck, there had been a massive die-off of rats. He also recalled that his Pasteur Institute colleague Paul Louis Simond told him that a number of Vietnamese wool factory workers contracted the plague after they were forced to sweep the floor clean of dead rats. Suddenly, the light turned on inside Yersin's head. He rushed back to the morgue; the floor was littered with dead rats. He ran to the worst-affected slums of the oldest parts of the city—the corpses of rats were everywhere. It all made sense. Thousands of years after it appeared, someone finally realized that rats were the key reservoir and vector for the plague. Yersin didn't know how rats communicated the plague, but he knew they did.

How didn't matter in the short term. Anti-rat measures such as trapping, poisoning, and habitat removal went into effect all over the world and the disease began to wane. When it was finally discovered that the fleas on the rats were the missing link, plague-reduction techniques changed. Because rat populations are so hard to control, many jurisdictions chose instead to control the fleas on them. Massive applications of insecticides do nothing to rats other than rid them of their parasites, but it can halt the progress of the plague. It's just easier to kill fleas than it is to kill rats. Although the last major outbreak was in Chile and Argentina in 1945, the

World Health Organization considered it a pandemic until 1959. The plague has been largely under control since then, with about two hundred deaths annually.

Pet-rat enthusiasts adamantly like to point out that it was the black rat that spread the plague through Europe and not the brown, which is almost invariably the type they keep. The logic behind this reasoning is that brown were not conclusively reported in Europe until 1727, after the most major outbreaks. But, while the black rat has been largely eliminated in the colder parts of the world and is almost never kept as a pet, the danger has never ceased and only declined through other methods with their absence. To say that the brown rat was not involved with the plague is a narrow-minded, even fanciful, opinion that totally discounts all but the most familiar plague outbreaks. A good argument could be made that the many millions who died of the plague in China and other parts of Asia (certainly as many as perished in Europe) contracted it from fleas that were riding around on the backs of brown rats. And there is no doubt that many of the cases encountered throughout the world since Yersin's discovery can be traced to the same brown rats many would portray as blameless.

Although better sanitation, massive applications of insecticides, and increased awareness have reduced the spread of plague to a comparative trickle, rats still carry other lethal diseases which are generally transmitted through bites. Chief among them is leptospirosis, also known as Weil's disease, named after Adolph Weil who, in 1886, isolated the bacteria. Although most cases are the result of bites, it can also be passed to humans through the ingestion of rat urine. Those stricken with the ailment suffer jaundice, an enlargement of the spleen, and a lack of proper kidney function. Preliminary symptoms include severe headaches, vomiting, muscle aches, and diarrhea. Without treatment, leptospirosis can result in meningitis, liver failure, or kidney failure, and such cases are fatal up to 40 percent of the time. There are no vaccines for leptospirosis, but treatment with antibiotics greatly reduces the risk of fatality. Even so, the World Health Organization reported 607 deaths from the disease, mostly in Latin America, in 2003. Besides plague and leptospirosis, rats are also known to spread typhus, spotted fever, trichinosis, tularemia, salmonella food poisoning, infectious jaundice, and other serious diseases to humans. There have been reliable reports of rats transmitting rabies, but it is very uncommon and has never happened in North America.

Despite its name, rat-bite fever is normally transmitted to humans through contact with rat urine via the mouth, eyes, or nose. Early symptoms of rat-bite fever, also known as Haverhill fever, include fever, chills, headache, and muscle pain. Over the next three days, the victim usually

Sick Making

Human fatality rates in diseases most frequently contracted from rats

Plague	10–95 percent
Hantavirus Pulmonary Syndrome	up to 40 percent
Eosinophilic Meningitis	1-35 percent
Leptospirosis	1–14 percent
Rat-bite fever	7–10 percent
Seoul virus	7 percent
Murine Typhus	<5 percent
Salmonella enterica serovar Typhimurium	<1 percent
Trichinosis	<1 percent

Sources: Centers for Disease Prevention and Control, American Academy of Family Physicians, University of South Carolina Medical School

suffers from a large-scale rash, particularly in the extremities. Later, any of the large joints may become swollen, red, and sore. If rat-bite fever goes without treatment, severe complications, including infection of the heart valves, may occur, and death results in about 10 percent of cases.

Of more concern to most North Americans than plague is hanta virus. A distant cousin of ebola, hanta virus (also known by the more descriptive name of hemorrhagic fever with renal syndrome) is a disease than is usually communicated to humans by rodents. But unlike most other rodent-borne diseases, which require a bite either from the animal or its fleas, hanta virus is usually inhaled when a human comes into contact with the urine, saliva, or feces of the mouse or rat. Since a healthy brown rat makes about two hundred droppings a day and urinates even more frequently, there's never a shortage of raw material.

Typically, a person will contract the disease when cleaning a rodent-affected area. By unintentionally stirring up droppings, nesting material, or even dust that has been urinated on, the virus becomes airborne through a process known as aerosolization and can be inhaled. Since cleaning up an area that has been housing rodents almost always results in releasing their waste material into the air, many people have become reluctant to maintain places where they congregate. Although still mainly a disease that affects China and the Korean peninsula, hanta virus can survive in any dry climate with a healthy rodent population and is increasingly common in the United States and Canada, particularly in the "four corners" states—Arizona, New Mexico, Utah, and Colorado.

The Alberta Agriculture ministry boasts about being "essentially rat-free since 1950," and has set up a 30-mile-deep buffer zone on its western and southern borders to prevent rats from entering, and has outlawed pet rats. "We maintain and broadcast our rat-free reputation, so that Albertans know that the province is free of rats," John B. Bourne, Alberta's Vertebrate Pest Specialist told *National Geographic*. "We have a network of people in cities and towns that are contact people should a citizen see a rat." Even so, Alberta has experienced more than a dozen infections and several deaths from hanta virus in recent years.

The disease is so frightening and so widespread that some historic buildings and even the visitor center at a national park (at Badlands in South Dakota) in the North American West have been closed to visitors because of the potential for exposure. Some ghost towns, which often house many rodents in their abandoned buildings, are surrounded by signs warning off visitors because of the likelihood of contracting the disease. The U.S. National Parks Service also instructs visitors to sites known to be infected with hanta virus—like California's Channel Islands—how to avoid rodents and protect themselves from disease.

Hanta virus in the United States is usually carried by deer mice—a cute little native species of mouse that ranges throughout the continent and is secretive enough to go largely unnoticed—but any rodent can play host, and brown rats are considered by health organizations the second most dangerous carrier. Of the 150,000 cases of hanta virus reported each year, anywhere from 0.5 to 45 percent fatality rates can be expected, depending on the seriousness of the infection. In most outbreaks, the death rate runs at around 2 percent. Hanta virus begins with fever, chills, muscle pains, headache, and gastrointestinal symptoms and is often mistaken for flu.

Since people who come into contact with rat urine or feces almost never see or smell it, hanta virus is often unde-tected until it matures and the patient's lungs fill with fluid and shortness of breath ensues—one survivor referred to the late stages as feeling like a "tight band around my chest and a pillow over my face." According to the Centers for Disease Control and Prevention in Atlanta, "there is no specific treat-ment, cure, or vaccine for hanta virus infection. However, we do know that if infected individuals are recognized early and receive medical attention in an intensive care unit, they may do better. In intensive care, patients are intubated [given arti-ficial breathing assistance] and given oxygen therapy to help them through the period of severe respiratory distress." They stress that it's important that anyone who suffers from flu-like symptoms let their doctor know if they may have been in contact with rodents or their droppings.

Disease isn't the only way humans can suffer from rat infestations. While city rats generally thrive on the constant flow of garbage created by humans, their country cousins often satisfy themselves with our crops and stored grain. David Pimental, a professor at Cornell University and the world's foremost expert on the effects of invasive species in the United States, estimates that rats cause about $19 billion (about the size of the entire gross domestic production of a country like Panama) agricultural damage to American farms every year.

According to Michael H. Glantz, director of the Environmental and Societal Impacts Group of the National Center for Atmospheric Research, farmers have pretty well given up on trying to prevent rats from eating their grain and have concentrated on growing so much that the portion rats take up won't be as sorely missed. "The lion's share of attention and research funds goes to improving crop yields and crop production," he said. "Considerably less goes to research on ways to reduce grain losses once they have been harvested and stored."

As protein seekers, rats prefer richer grain and will often eat only the more nutritious seed embryo, ignoring the rest of the grain and exponentially increasing the total amount of affected product as they travel from kernel to kernel, eating only their favorite part.

Far more damaging than what they eat is what they spoil. Feeding rats urinate and defecate on much more grain than they eat. While rats might not mind eating grain with a few of their own feces thrown in, humans do. And not just because they're squeamish. According to the International Rice Research Institute, rat urine and droppings can carry as many as fifty diseases that can be communicated to humans or livestock. Luckily, rat urine glows under some forms of ultraviolet light, which makes it relatively easy to detect. But since there is no effective way of cleaning rat-affected grain, it must be declared unfit for human or animal consumption and disposed of. The International Rice Research Institute estimated in 1999 that the amount of rice lost to rats in nine East Asian countries each year could match the total caloric requirements of about 362 million people.

Besides the grain itself, farmers must also contend with the infrastructure damage rats do in their efforts to get at protected grain, including: grain leaks from damaged bags or storage containers; stacks of bags collapsing due to damage to the lower layers; silos and warehouses which may subside or even collapse as a result of rats gnawing entrance holes in lower levels; and irrigation systems and drainage canals which can be ruined as rats build nests in their sides. "It almost doesn't make sense to try to protect grain from rats," said Ryan, a Southern Ontario corn farmer. "The more you invest to keep them out, the more equipment they ruin—they always get their share—you might as well just invite them in." Walking around his farm, Ryan pointed out rat holes in the ground, the bases of doors, fences and walls that have been gnawed to gain entry and tools and implements with handles that have been chewed out of usefulness. "They love anything you've been working with," he told me. "The sweat from your hands impregnates wood or rubber with salt and the rats chew it up to eat the salt." Every part of his farm seems crisscrossed with little trails of stamped-down grass. Ryan does everything he can to reduce the number of rats on his farm, but it doesn't do much good. Their numbers appear to fluctuate, he says, with his efforts, but "even if I managed to kill every rat in a 50-mile radius, new ones would move in before I could get rid of their bodies."

The tour ended when Ryan lifted up a piece of plywood. The horde of rats underneath, temporarily blinded by the sunlight, ran around and into each other in the confusion— the overall effect was that of a bubbling, flowing carpet of brownish-gray fur. Before he dropped the plywood, the rats dispersed in a thousand different directions. "I hate 'em," he said. "But they are part of the business." I asked him if the often-repeated statistic that about a third of all grain grown is either eaten or contaminated by rats. "That seems a bit high," he said after what appeared to be a lot of serious thought. "But definitely in the ballpark."

When rats aren't eating our grain, they are eating our poultry. Invasive rats long ago replaced native predators in many parts of the world as the greatest natural threat to the livestock held by poultry farmers. Although most farmed birds are now individually caged and generally safe from direct predation (free-range chickens, on the other hand, are sometimes exposed to hunting rats, particularly at night), rats still cause a great amount of damage to the industry. Protein-rich poultry feed is as nutritious and palatable for rats as it is for chickens and rats consume a great deal of it and contaminate far more with their excretions. Rat infestations also cause major damage to poultry farms as ambitious rats try to figure out ways to get at the feed or even at the birds, damaging infrastructure in efforts to get closer. Even the mere presence of rats can kill poultry. Chickens, which also originated in Southeast Asia, instinctively recognize rats as predators and invariably attempt to flee when they are around. According to the British Department of Environment, Food and Rural Affairs: "Rats can create panic and hysteria in flocks and can give rise to sudden, heavy mortality losses due to smothering." Chickens fear rats so intensely that the mere smell of them can create a lethal riot. Poultry researchers like to retell the story of the chicken farmer in Mississippi who found what he thought was a rat dropping among his birds. Although he had encountered no other signs of infestation, he wanted to get rid of the rats because he intended to sell the farm. After three months, he'd killed 1800 rats and gotten out of the chicken business to become an exterminator.

While infestations on farms do much more damage, the thought of rats in restaurants is, much more disturbing. Unless its staff is very diligent about rat prevention, a restaurant is even more likely to house uninvited guests than a residence would be. Rats are attracted to restaurants mainly because of the huge amounts of food—not just what's in storage, but the constant flow of garbage rich in prepared dishes often high in fat and protein. Even the most disciplined kitchen staffs make messes and everyone gets a bit sloppy when they're overwhelmed by lunch or dinner rushes. What looks like a simple grease spill to a person looks like Christmas morning to a rat family.

The people who make and enforce hygiene standards are aware of what attracts rats and work very hard to make sure that the effects of carelessness, short staffing, and poor design are minimized in the restaurant industry. Of course, how well these rules are followed varies wildly from place to place and are traditionally prone to bribery and other forms of corruption. One of the truly hardworking members of the community is Reg Ayre, manager of the Healthy Environment division of Toronto Public Health. Originally from South Africa, Ayre admits he's seen some massive infestations in his time and that what he sees in Toronto is actually pretty tame by the standards of some places he's been. But that doesn't mean the city is free of rats, and he maintains that only the use of "very rigid inspection standards" keep their numbers down.

No major city is ever truly rat free, and people like Ayre are constantly looking for signs—whether they are on duty or not. "To me, it's obvious when rats are about—you can see gnaw marks, often resulting in structural damage, and since they urinate and defecate all over, the smell is usually a dead giveaway," Ayre said. Most obvious, he reminded me—"if there are enough of them and they've gone unmolested for a while"—are the grease trails where their fur has rubbed against a wall.

Many diners miss these telltale signs because they simply aren't looking for them. Sometimes, however, the presence of rats is so obvious that everybody knows. People who were eating at the food court in the Chinatown Centre, a downtown Toronto shopping mall in June 2005, called Toronto Public Health, and some of Ayre's team went to investigate. Jim Chan, the food-safety manager at the scene, is a skilled and experienced officer, but what he saw at the mall required none of his savvy. "We saw live evidence of rat infestations," said Chan, with a politician's flair for understatement. He then added: "There was a live rat in the food court area." Immediately, the food-preparation and dining areas were cordoned off, and mall staff armed with bleach and disinfectants were dispatched.

Although rat infestations occur everywhere in the world, Africa seems to get hit harder than anywhere else these days. Dr. Steve Belmain, of the British National Resources Institute, studies rats and their effect on people in places like Mozambique. People in his area of study "have consistently identified that rats are one of the primary post-harvest problems, consuming and contaminating stored food such as rice, groundnuts (peanuts) and maize (corn)," he said. "Rats are a constant problem because they affect crops, both in store and in the field. They also cause damage to buildings, eating and contaminating livestock feed, killing poultry and eating their eggs."

One of the biggest problems in much of East Africa, it would seem, is the abundance of homes with thatched roofs. As discussed earlier, rats easily create burrows in the thatching and as many as a hundred may occupy the roof of an average-size home, far outnumbering humans and con-

suming an estimated 900 pounds of food in each household every year. Worse even than the food that rats eat are
the diseases they bring. "Rat waste literally rains down on
people while they sleep—it gets into the water and the
food," said Belmain. Not only is plague constantly present
in the area, but the rats are "closely associated with other
diseases such as leptospirosis and can rapidly spread other
gastroenteric diseases such as cholera and salmonella,"
said Belmain. "In addition, approximately 10 percent of
people are regularly bitten by rats while they are sleeping,
leading to secondary infections and rat-bite fevers from bacteria entering the wounds."

Rat populations have boomed in Mozambique as decades
of war, years of drought, and the resulting poverty among
humans have rid the former Portuguese colony of any effective predators. The people in the area are willing to fight back
but often find themselves underequipped. "Existing knowledge and technology on rodent control is, in most cases,
inappropriate for the control of rats in rural villages," said
Belmain. "Rodenticides are not an option as such toxicants
are usually too expensive, not readily available and likely to be
used incorrectly."

With poisoning out of the question, Belmain and the villagers have reduced rat populations initially with preventive
methods. Their first targets were the thatched roofs.
Traditionally, thatching was replaced every year, but when
farmers did it more often, they notice a drastic reduction in
the number of rats in their homes. Even better results were
achieved when the thatching was removed and metal or other
materials were used instead. With most potential nesting
sites removed, the team made an effort to deprive the

animals of food and water. "Covering drinking-water vessels limits water resources available to rodents, as well as reducing disease transmission," said Belmain. "Placing waste and rubbish away from households and clearing vegetation to a distance of 10 meters or more should also help to reduce numbers of rodents."

While those efforts have shown good results, they pale in comparison to the success the team saw with trapping. In most places in the world, trapping isn't very successful because it's a labor-intensive task and neophobic rats can quickly become trap-shy. But the Mozambican farmers Belmain was working with turned out to be eager and innovative trappers. Those households which engaged in active trapping saw rat populations drop 50 to 70 percent faster than those that didn't. Perhaps even more significantly, after a year of trapping, the size of the average rat caught was about half the size of those caught when trapping began.

The Mozambican farmers had another reason to prefer trapping—you can't eat a poisoned rat. In discussions with the farmers, Belmain learned that rats were the primary source of protein for many families in the area. While rats are generally pretty nutritious, especially in diets lacking other sources of protein, those in East Africa present a genuine risk, as they are more likely to carry disease than those in other parts of the world. And many of the diseases carried by rats can be communicated by eating their meat. The people know the dangers of rat hunting, but the meat is just too valuable to their dietary needs. Four young men ranging in ages from eight to about fourteen who identified themselves as the Xavier brothers told a BBC news crew that they knew they were exposing themselves to

plague and other diseases, but that rats were the only animals left in the countryside to hunt.

They kill us and we kill them. Since both humans and
rats are currently undergoing unbridled population explo-
sions, the competition has to be declared a draw. The
life-and-death competition between rats and humans has, of
course, led to a great deal of animosity over the years. In the
Atharva Veda, a Hindu sacred text that dates back to about
2200 BC, there is a curse on rats:

O, Ashwini. Kill the burrowing rodents that devastate
our food grains. Slice their hearts, break their necks,
plug their mouths so that they cannot destroy our food.

It didn't work. Neither did any of the other countless
curses, indictments, trials, and even politely worded letters
people have addressed to deities or to the rats themselves
over the centuries. They won't leave our homes or places of
business no matter how, or how, often we ask.

Natural Rat Traps

As the plague spread through London in 1664, the Lord Mayor signed an order to destroy dogs and cats. In his book *Journal of the Plague Years*, Daniel Defoe estimated that 40,000 dogs and 200,000 cats were slaughtered. The removal of these predators allowed rats to roam the streets more freely and greatly hastened the spread of the disease. Although dogs and cats can contract plague, there has never been a record of a human receiving plague from contact with either animal.

Sources: Britain Express, Centers for Disease Control and Prevention

Entertainer, Test Subject, and Family Friend

Maura insists I call her "Raven." She weighs, by my rough estimate, about 260 pounds. She's maybe five foot three and has numerous piercings in her ears, nose, eyebrow, lips, tongue, and God knows where else. She proudly shows me the tattoos—mostly of fanciful creatures and magical-type people—on her arms, shoulders, and back. She also takes a great deal of pride in showing me the pet rat on her shoulder. She was surprised when I stopped to talk to her ("You look so normal" is her disdainful and somewhat suspicious assessment of me), but very intrigued when she found out that I was writing a book about her favorite animal.

Her rat looks nervous up there on her shoulder, pacing around and lifting its two front paws alternatively, like a dog waiting for its dinner. He's not real big, smaller than most of the wild rats I've seen, and the front part of his body is a kind of chocolate brown while the back part is pure white. Those markings, I'm told, make him a "bareback hooded." After speaking with Raven about some of her other interests and beliefs, I'm not terribly surprised to learn his name is Lucifer.

We were sitting together on a busy Toronto sidewalk as some of Raven's friends milled around and occasionally asked passersby for spare change. When Raven takes her turn at panhandling, she always makes sure one of her friends is holding the rat. "People just aren't ready for him," she said. "There's something about rats that most of your mainstream-type people, no offense to you of course, don't understand."

She asked me if I wanted to hold him. "Sure," I said, and I could tell she was a little bit disappointed that I wasn't scared or freaked out—reactions I think she'd like from people most of the time. Lucifer sat almost contentedly in my left hand. It's a really strange feeling, holding a rat. The collapsible rib cage gives them a springy, almost gelatinous feel, nothing like a more rigidly built puppy or kitten the same size. For most of my time with a rat in my hands, the only thing I could think about was how overwhelmingly fragile he felt, like if I held him any tighter it would squish the very life out of him. I knew intellectually it wasn't true, but I couldn't shake the feeling and I never knew if I was holding him too tightly or not firmly enough.

After a while, he made it clear he wasn't overly comfortable with me. His front paws were quickly on my index finger and he was pushing upward with what appeared to me to be overdramatic motions. I knew he could easily escape my gentle grasp if he thought he was any danger, so his behavior seemed more like an almost passive-aggressive admonition to hold him the right way rather than an attempt to flee. In an effort to calm him down, I stroked his little head and shoulders with my right hand and spoke to him. I'm a dog person, so the first thing that occurred to me was: "Who's a pretty rat then?" Those of Raven's friends who did not laugh at me looked on in horror. She asked for Lucifer back. I guess I'm just not, as she said, a rat person.

But Raven most certainly is. Like all the other rat owners I've met, she explains that she likes rats because they are smart, affectionate, and clean. And, like all the others, she's adamant about these claims. Rat owners love to talk about their pets and use the word "extremely" more than any group of people I've ever met. Their rats are "extremely" clean, "extremely" affectionate, "extremely" intelligent, and "extremely" cute, among other extreme claims.

And, like many of the other rat owners I spoke with, Raven eventually admitted that she wanted a rat for a pet because she identified with them. People who keep rats as pets tend to look on rats as terribly misunderstood, hated for no good reason other than being rats. And, from my experience, rat owners often look at themselves in much the same way. I hate to paint an entire group with such a wide brush, but I have met, interviewed, talked to, e-mailed with, chatted with or read about more than a hundred individual rat owners and they really didn't differ all that much in their reasons for choosing their pets.

All would be in some way or another considered eccentric, usually proudly so. All had strong, usually antiestablishment, political views that they were pleased to share. Many had tattoos, piercings, or other look-at-me adornments.

Many expressed an interest in science fiction, fantasy and/or medieval times. Many were vegetarians. Many talked with cutesy jargon, referring to rats as "ratties," mice as "meeses," and rabbits as "wabbits." Many were engaged in noncommercial art and all made clear their disdain of mainstream culture—often and without any solicitation. I'm not saying that every rat owner has these qualities, just every one of the hundred or so I ran into, usually while under the guise of a prospective or novice rat owner looking for advice.

The ones I met fell into two basic groups: the minority were like Raven, those who had rats to scare or freak out people (usually their parents) and those who had rats as an affected display of their kindness to society's least-loved creature. Typically, that subgroup of rat owners would speak of themselves in congratulatory tones, as though owning a pet rat were some kind of moral victory. "When you can appreciate the small things in life, like a rat, a dirty rat, you can appreciate anything," said Joanne "Bella" Hodges, president of the Florida Rat Club and an artist who draws and paints rat-themed images.

Like all pets, rats generally have names that reflect their owner's personality. While the rats in Lucifer's litter received names like Damien, Anthrax, Bela, Bubonic, and Aleister, most rat owners go with adorable rather than fearsome—I've encountered Woowoo, Moopie, Scruffles, Skweekers, dozens of names that end with "z" and countless others with names based on puns using the word "rat" or, just as often, "wat." On the American Fancy Rat and Mouse Association website, the name on their sample rat registry certificate is "KK Likkity." And you can buy your purebred pets from ratteries (rat farms) with names like the Spoiled Ratten, Lil' Ratscals,

Rodents of Unusual Sweetness, Noble Gaian Rat Republic, KuddlyKorner4U, or Manitou Mischief. Most people who own rat farms claim to be not in the business for profit, but rather for the love of rats.

Although they can all be included into one of two distinct groups, the common thread among rat owners I encountered was that they all considered themselves highly, if not extraordinarily, intelligent and wildly unappreciated.

Rats themselves do make pretty decent pets, as rodents go. Virtually all pet rats are brown rats, as the breed is smarter, more social, and less nocturnal than black rats. A few generally very experienced rat fanciers keep black rats, but they are very rare. Pet rats are certainly smarter, more inquisitive, and more social—particularly with humans—than hamsters, guinea pigs, gerbils, chinchillas, and mice, the other commonly held rodents. And, given proper socialization, they are pretty docile; far from the vicious reputation they have in the wild. "They're as different from wild rats as wolves are from dogs," said Debbie Ducommun, founder of the Rat Fan Club and a woman who answers her home phone by saying "Hello, Rat Lady." Humane societies generally agree with her. Lost, abandoned, and unwanted pet rats are treated with the same respect and kindness as dogs or cats. "For us, the problem with rats in the field is knowing which ones are pets and which are wild," said a humane society employee I know. "But if someone brings us a rat or calls us about one in trouble, it's only natural that it has the same rights as any other pet."

Despite what their owners say, I didn't find the rats I was exposed to particularly clean, although since they do groom themselves frequently their bodies themselves are rarely dirty. The problem is that they are pretty relaxed about where they leave their excretions. In fact, the males urinate pretty well everywhere, leaving drops behind them as they explore, and it has a particularly virulent scent. It's a good idea to change a pet rat's bedding and litter frequently to keep the smell down, but too many cleanings can have the reverse effect. Presented with an unfamiliar-smelling environment, a rat will make itself feel more confident by urinating enough so that it becomes familiar enough for the rat's comfort. Rat feces aren't quite as smelly. Since a good-sized rat, as we have seen, can leave two hundred droppings a day, they can mount up very quickly. But since rats do generally like to defecate in a designated area, cleaning it up isn't a huge task. Rats also chew every chance they get, which can create a lot of debris and damaged items.

As far as the claims of extreme intelligence and extreme affection are concerned, the rat's beauty is definitely in the eye of the beholder. I've frequently been told "they're smarter than dogs," but that claim stretches credibility way beyond the breaking point. Rats can be taught rudimentary behaviors like recognizing their names or traversing through obstacle courses, but even those tricks require great patience from the human, and rats show little else beyond that. Many of their owner's claims of intelligence seem to me to be more accurately described as alertness (a beneficial trait for a prey species), rather than actual intellect.

And rats can be sort of affectionate in that they will begin to enjoy coming into contact with their owners. They readily accept stroking from familiar humans and occasionally lick them. Pet rats eventually learn to greet their human keepers with nuzzling and bruxing—an audible grinding of the teeth that rat enthusiasts liken to a cat's purring. It sounds exactly as you'd expect.

Rat owners, at least the ones I've met, never tire of pointing out how their pets compare to other animals. They don't slobber, they don't get hair balls, they don't scratch furniture, and they don't try to mate with your leg. The only drawback any ever admitted to me is the rat's short lifespan, usually no more than two years, although some have lived for seven years. "You only start to get to know them when they die on you," said Raven.

I tend to agree with Raven's assertion that there are rat people and non–rat people. Every person I encountered who had a pet rat treated it with dignity, respect, and sincere affection. They love them as a non–rat person might love a dog or cat. My experience has shown that there's a simple test to determine whether you are a rat person or not. Simply look at a pet rat. Look at its naked tail, its outsized testicles, and its face that can only be described as rat-like. If you don't see vermin, you're probably a rat person.

Keeping rats as pets is a relatively new phenomenon. And it evolved from an entirely different practice. The world used to be a far more barbaric place, even just a few generations ago. Before the onset of mass media, people had other ways to entertain themselves and let off steam, often violently. Historian William Manchester, in *A World Lit Only by Fire*, his excellent account of the medieval world, tells of the popular practice of nailing live cats to boards—a hobby particularly enjoyed by children.

Perhaps derived from the Roman Coliseum but more likely evolving from random violence to animals, Europeans became fascinated by what were known as blood sports—games which virtually always led to the violent death of an animal. Some—like hunting, fishing, bullfighting, and cockfighting—exist today with varying degrees of public acceptance. One of the most popular of all blood sports was "baiting"—a euphemism for forcing animals to fight each other to the death. Other than horses, which were deemed far too valuable to risk, pretty well any animal could be thrown into a pit and forced to defend itself, often with prodding from humans to get the violence started. Animals with a little fight in them—particularly bulls, bears, and badgers—were extremely popular.

As the sport evolved, baiters found that their fans preferred to see fights in which dogs, either alone or in packs, fought against other animals. It made sense for the baiters, too. Dogs are not only the most effective killers of all the familiar animals, but even the most vicious dog can be easily handled by its owner because of its deeply ingrained hierarchical behavior. As the popularity of baiting grew, various dogs were bred specifically for baiting, often with features or traits matching their gruesome tasks. The Old English bulldog, for example, may look cute, even ridiculous by today's standards, but its flat face, long canines, loose skin and solid robust body were developed for tearing bulls fifty times their weight to pieces.

As with many sports, the real interest for many spectators and the real money for baiting organizers lay in betting. But since the dogs always won, there wasn't much to bet on and most baits became exhibitions until a new star was found. In urban areas, rats were very common and rarely killed with much effectiveness. Regarded by most people as little more than a nuisance, rats were fairly easy to catch if a person was determined enough, but their sheer numbers and amazing reproductive powers prevented any effective population control. Captive rats were thrust into baiting pits by the hundreds. Rat baiting was a fairly simple game. Rat pits, usually in the cellars of taverns, were generally 8 foot square, about 4 foot deep and lined with highly polished tin to prevent the rats from escaping. In rat baiting's earliest incarnations, two dogs were set in the pit and the winner was determined by whose dog killed more rats. But in the utter chaos of the ensuing melee, it was often hard to be sure which dog killed which rat. When money's on the line, judgment calls are frowned upon. Under pressure from bettors, the game changed and the rats were pitted (a word that originated from baiting) against a single dog.

An enterprising journalist named Dennis Tilden Lynch attended a rat bait in New York City in 1871 and described it in horrifying detail. In an effort to build suspense, the organizers allowed the spectators a chance to watch the frightened and confused rats for a while. Two men, supposed to be nonaligned with the host or any bettors, dropped a hundred rats from canvas bags into the pit:

> For a full five minutes there is a craning of necks as the rats scurry around the bottom of the pit, vainly seeking escape...this five minute period enables all concerned to inspect the rats, for each one must be sound. The occasional weak or injured rat is removed with a tongs and another substituted. The [dog's] handler watches the frantically weaving mass beneath, for when the word is given, he must drop the dog on the patch of floor where the fewest rats are at that important moment.

When given the signal, the handler threw his dog into the pit. Terriers, specifically bred to hunt small, burrowing mammals, were preferred. Originally, the best ratters were Manchester terriers—small black-and-tan dogs with electric reflexes—but they were later superseded by specially bred rat terriers. Scarcely larger than the rats they massacred, rat terriers (also known as feists for their fiery dispositions) have sharp teeth, strong jaws, and massively powerful necks. Those characteristics came in handy, as the terrier would grab a rat in its jaws, give it a quick shake to break its neck, then move on to the next.

Sensing that escape was impossible, the rats would eventually turn on their tormentor, but it didn't do much good against these tough little dogs. According to Lynch, "There are moments when the dog is barely visible as rats fasten themselves to his face, ears, head, neck and legs. Save for an occasional shake, the dog ignores the fang-fastened rodents for their hold is brief." Rats killed by other rats in the frenzy were also counted in the dog's score. A very good rat terrier could rid the pit of its hundred rats in about a half hour, although a champion named Jack Underhill (handled by a young man named Billy Fagan) once managed the feat in eleven and a half minutes, or less than seven seconds per dead rat. A London-based terrier, named Jocko the Wonder Dog, is said to have done it in five minutes and twenty-eight seconds, but that seems to me like an exaggeration.

Rat terriers became popular pets in Britain, and were introduced to the United States by Teddy Roosevelt, who learned about them when he was New York City's chief of police and owned two of them while he was president. Some American breeders, perhaps of the opinion that people may think the dogs are called rat terriers because they look like rats, now market them under the name Teddy Roosevelt terriers.

Rat baiting was so popular that rat catching became a profession and even launched its own stars. By the middle of the 19th century, genteel types usually wanted their houses free of rats as a show of cleanliness, and farmers wanted them gone because of the amount of grain rats consumed. But unlike today's exterminators, rat catchers tried to keep their rats alive to supply the baiting circuit. "I've had as many as two thousand rats in this very house at one time," said Jimmy Shaw, a London rat catcher in the 1850s who was an expert at marketing his skill. "They'll consume a sack of barley meal a week, and the brutes, if you don't give 'em good stuff, they'll eat one another, hang 'em!"

Typically, a man or boy from the lower classes would be hired to stick his hand into a hole or haystack, feel around for rats, pull them out and place them in a bag. Gloves were not used as they reduced the rat catcher's ability to feel for rats and, since they were paid by the rat, production was deemed more important than safety at a time when the poor were not always treated much better than animals. Bites were common, but rat catchers developed calluses in frequently bitten spots and soldiered on as best they could.

"A rat's bite is very singular, it's a three-cornered one, like a leech's, only deeper, of course, and it will bleed for ever such a time," said Shaw. "My boys have sometimes had their fingers go dreadfully bad from rat bites, so that they turn all black and putrid-like—aye, as black as the horse-hair covering to my sofa. People have said to me: 'You ought to send the lad to the hospital, and have his finger took off' but I've always left it to the lads, and they've said, 'Oh, don't mind it, father; it'll get all right by and by.' And so it has." It was a dangerous business with a very high casualty rate.

But as expert as Shaw was, he was a small-timer compared to the great Jack Black, who billed himself as "Rat and Mole Destroyer to Her Majesty." When not ridding Victoria's palaces of rodents and burrowing insectivores, Black traveled the country in a cart painted with lurid depictions of rats and he wore an outrageous self-designed scarlet uniform with a huge leather belt inlaid with cast-iron rats. When he stopped in a town or neighborhood, he set up a stage and put on a show. He handled rats, "as though they were blind kittens," according to one observer.

"Here I saw him dip his hand into this cage of rats and take out as many as he could hold, a feat which generally caused an 'oh!' of wonder to escape from the crowd, especially when they observed that his hands were unbitten," said Henry Mayhew in his classic book, *London Labour and the London Poor.*

"Women more particularly shuddered when they beheld him place some half-dozen of the dusty-looking brutes within his shirt next to his skin; and men swore the animals had been tamed, as he let them run up his arms like squirrels, and the people gathered round beheld them sitting on his shoulders cleaning their faces with their front-paws, or rising up on their hind legs like little kangaroos, and sniffing about his ears and cheeks." At a time when the concept of a domesticated rat was almost incomprehensible, Black got away with the fabrication that the rats had been captured that day from nearby sewers and that it was his unique ability that tamed them. At that point, he sold poisons and traps to his astounded audience.

Despite his occupation of killing rats and his occasional habit of eating them fried in butter, Black had a fondness for rats and he kept many of them, along with sparrows (he called them "the rats of the bird world"), ferrets, and terriers as pets. Besides catching rats, Black also ran a taxidermy shop and, for a brief time, a tavern where his daughter, who worked behind the bar, wore a red velvet dress with the words "Rat Catcher's Daughter" stitched on the bodice.

Black happened upon his greatest success, and thus his place in history, by accident. One night, while passing through a graveyard, he saw a pure white rat (which we would recognize today as an albino). He stalked and captured it and brought it home as a pet. When he took it along on his tours, he noticed that it quickly became the star of the show and that people, particularly young women, frequently offered to buy it from him. Rather than sell his prized rat, he decided to breed it in hopes of creating more white rats. Since albinism is an inherited trait, his plan was a success. Before long, Black was selling white, spotted, and hooded rats to "young ladies" and they became a modest fad among the privileged classes. Beatrix Potter, author of the beloved Peter Rabbit series, is said to have bought a rat from Black and based her 1908 book, *The Tale of Samuel Whiskers,* on her pet of the same name. Even Queen Victoria is said to have kept two in gilded cages. Many scientists and rat fanciers alike believe virtually all pet rats are in some way related to the single albino that Black found in the graveyard.

But it wasn't until 1901 that rats gained wide acceptance as pets in England. A young woman named Mary Douglas wrote a letter asking the National Mouse Club (comparatively harmless mice have been kept as pets a bit longer than rats) if she could join with her hooded rat. They agreed and Douglas entered her in a competition sponsored by the NMC in the London suburb of Aylesbury and won best in show. She coined the phrase "fancy rats" to differentiate pets from wild rats and formed the Fancy Rats association, which standardized "breeds" and held competitions. She also named the concept of keeping as "rat fancy," using the English slang term "fancy" to mean have affection for—as in "I fancy that rat." She was so successful in promoting rats that the NMC merged with her club in 1912, becoming the National Rat and Mouse Club (NRMC). But the popularity of pet rats went into drastic decline in 1921 when the charismatic Douglas died. By 1929, the NRMC dropped Rats from its title and reverted to the NMC, which still exists today.

Very few people kept rats as pets over the next few decades, but in the 1960s—when eccentric behavior was again widely celebrated—they began to come back into vogue in some circles. Pet books of the era suggested that would-be rat owners contact laboratories for young rats, as there were virtually never sold in stores. In 1976, the National Fancy Rat Society was formed in England and two years later the Mouse and Rat Breeders Association appeared in the U.S. Since then, pet rats have gained steadily in numbers and public acceptance.

While there are about a half-million rat-owning households in North America according to the Rat Assistance & Teaching Society, many people are still against the idea, often because they believe that escaped pet rats may start infestations where none exist. Alberta, which claims to be free of wild rats, has a long-standing ban of pet rats. In 2005, the neighboring province of Saskatchewan, which has a wild-rat problem, was considering a similar ban, and rat fancier organizations around the world mobilized. An online petition against the ban drew more than eight hundred signatures. Most of the signatories who left comments appeared (from their writing) to be children, and the distinct majority used idioms and slang more closely associated with England or Australia, places where the practice of keeping pet rats is more widely accepted, than with the Canadian Prairies.

Virtually all of the comprehensible responses maintained that pet rats could never survive in the wild long enough to start an infestation—although I know dozens of biologists, particularly in places like New Zealand and the Falkland Islands, who would like (perhaps violently) to dissuade them from that opinion. Those who claim that their beloved pets would die almost immediately after they left their cages—which would be the only scenario under which they wouldn't have enough time to reproduce—often compare pet rats to dogs and wild rats to wolves without realizing what a bad idea that is. Feral dogs, the descendants of domestic dogs that have escaped or been set free, are the world's widest-ranging and most numerous wild canines and do far and away the most damage. Where they exist in numbers, feral dogs do a remarkable amount of damage to

Picky Eaters

Wild rats' favorite foods

Scrambled eggs
Macaroni and cheese
Cooked corn
Cooked potatoes
Cooked oatmeal
Cooked sweet potatoes
Bread
Raw corn
Raw beef
Raw sweet potatoes
Corned beef
Cooked chicken
Bananas
Cooked carrots

Source: "A Preliminary Analysis of Garbage as Food for the Norway Rat," Martin W. Schein

pets, wildlife, livestock, and even crops like low-growing fruits. Everywhere they occur, feral dogs form packs and hunt and harass domestic animals and are unparalleled in their killing ability. Feral dog predation can result in huge losses of livestock as their attacks promote hysteria, abortions and premature births in the animals they don't kill. Even a well-fed pack of feral dogs will kill any animal they encounter, just for the excitement. Feral dogs that can't find a pack simply adjust their hunting technique to a coyote-like style, stalking and pouncing on smaller prey. They can also cause immense amounts of indirect damage as they bring new and strange diseases to vulnerable environments. While mange is an easily treatable skin condition many pets face and overcome with a few shampoos, it can be lethal in wild animals and has played havoc with North America's populations of foxes, wolves and coyotes. Feral dogs also impact native canines with their habit of interbreeding with them. Coyote–dog mixes are commonplace in areas where both animals exist and interbreeding with feral dogs brought the number of purebred red wolves in their last isolated population so low that they were all trapped and moved from the swamps of Texas and Louisiana to dog-free islands off the Atlantic coast of North Carolina. Packs of feral dogs with as many as 150 members roam the mountains of Bosnia-Herzegovina and keep the people from wandering in their turf, a pack of feral dogs killed an 86-year-old woman in Rochefort, France, in 2000 and in 1999 no less an authority than the American Journal of Forensic Medicine and Pathology published an article called "Dog Pack Attack: Hunting Humans," which details how feral dogs can lose their bond with humans and view them as competitors or even prey. Where they are not strictly controlled with zero tolerance policies, feral dogs are as dangerous and damaging as, well, rats. While rat fanciers may get a lot of mileage out of comparing their pets to the lovable family pup, they may not want to bring up the whole harmless-as-a-feral-dog thing.

At about the same time rats began to come into our homes as pets, they made their way into our laboratories. The earliest reference to rats used in scientific experiments dates to 1828, and rats were commonly being used for breeding and genetic experiments by 1880. One population, at the Jardin des Plantes (botanical garden) in Paris, has been successfully inbred since 1856. Ironically, the same complex housed a wild-rat population so large and bold that novelist George Orwell reported in 1928 that they could be fed by hand.

Realizing the advantage of experimenting on rats, many laboratories caught wild ones or bought them from a new generation of rat catchers, usually children, who were paid only for healthy-looking rats. But their tendency to inflict painful, sometimes disease-ridden bites led scientists to look for a more docile creature. Successful breeding led to a desire to maintain a genetically similar strain of rats, to help improve the accuracy of experimentation. In 1906, a neurologist named Henry Donaldson, working at an independent medical research laboratory, the Wistar Institute in Philadelphia, was the first to produce a standardized rat which they described as "mildly prolific and resistant to spontaneous tumors." Other labs, especially Sprague–Dawley Farms of Wisconsin, have come up with other breeds, but Wistar rats are still considered the industry standard and the majority of lab rats alive today can trace their lineage to Dr. Donaldson's albinos.

People use the term "guinea pig" as a metaphor for experimental subject, and while the concept of a white mouse in a maze is commonplace enough to be a cliché, rats have traditionally far outnumbered any other creature in scientific study. A wide variety of inbred and mutated rats—including hairless varieties bred to make skin tumors and other irregularities easier to observe—are available to experimenters from scientific supply houses like Ace Animals of Boyertown, Pennsylvania. Their rats are guaranteed unable to vomit and, they promise, "Cannibalism is uncommon." Online ordering is simple, and prices range from $8.50 for babies to $68 for a pregnant female.

But even these well-established strains may go out of style soon as researchers are developing computer-based models of lab animals. In May 2005, the American Diabetes Foundation and Entelos, a biopharmaceutical firm, developed a virtual mouse for researchers to experiment upon. The use of computer-based virtual specimens is still in its infancy, but there is a growing trend towards using them rather than the estimated eighteen million animals who die in labs every year. And there are scientists who are anxious to proceed with virtual animals and not just for the sake of live subjects. Many experts have come to believe that while humans and rats share an astounding number of physical similarities, they aren't interchangeable when it comes to health, especially in their reactions to drugs. "Animal research is just not valid in understanding how drugs apply to humans," said Dr. John Pippin, a Dallas-based cardiologist and former animal researcher. "It has often proven to be misleading and potentially dangerous for the evaluation of drugs that will be prescribed for humans." Most governing bodies, like the U.S. Food and Drug Administration, require that all drugs be tested on animals before they are approved for humans. That's unlikely to change unless there is a major swing in scientists' and politicians' thinking as regards animal testing and virtual models.

Although never truly farmed except for the pet trade and as pet food, rats do, however, wind up on dinner plates around the world. In the West, stories of humans eating rats are almost invariably associated with men or women who find themselves starving, desperate, and unable to locate any other food (or at least protein) sources. The concept was delightfully discussed in "Blackadder Goes Forth" the Rowan Atkinson comedy about British soldiers in the trenches of France during World War I:

> Captain Blackadder: What's on the menu?
> Private Baldrick: Rat. Sauté or fricassee.
> Captain Blackadder: Oh, the agony of choice. Sauté involves?
> Private Baldrick: Well, you take the freshly shaved rat, and you marinade it in a puddle for a while.
> Captain Blackadder: Hmm, for how long?
> Private Baldrick: Until it's drowned. Then you stretch it out under a hot light bulb, then you get within dashing distance of the latrine, and then you scoff it right down.
> Captain Blackadder: So that's sautéing, and fricasseeing?
> Private Baldrick: Exactly the same, just a slightly bigger rat.

History is rife with accounts of people who have faced desperate situations (most often as prisoners, on long ocean voyages, or after a shipwreck) and have eaten rats as a last resort. When former political prisoner and torture victim Lee Soon-ok testified before a U.S. House International Relations Committee about conditions in a North Korean prison camp she had been held in, she spoke of horrible executions, regular torture, forced labor, and constant starvation. "They say it is a day of great fortune if a prisoner finds a rat creeping up from the bottom of the toilet hole," she said. "The prisoners catch it with their bare hands and devour it raw, as rats are the only source of meat in the prison. They say the wonderful taste of a raw rat is unforgettable. If they are caught eating a rat, however, the punishment is extended. So they have to be very careful when catching and eating a rat."

But, according to Belmain, who has seen rat consumption grow markedly in East Africa as other species have disappeared and local people are becoming more proficient at rat hunting, "Many African and Asian societies eat rats normally." Rats have become indisputably popular with many people. A number of shopkeepers in British and French cities have been charged with offenses derived from importing "bush meat"—the flesh of wild animals—for African immigrants looking for a taste of home. The first of them, a Tottenham, England, grocer named Paulina Owusu Pepra was found guilty of twenty-three offenses and sentenced to three months in prison in 2004 after officials found tons of decomposing bush meat in her shop. Most of it was rat. "Pepra had the shop for several years and she had been warned on many occasions but always ignored the warnings," said Dr. Yunes Teinaz, the senior environmental officer for the area. "I believe she has smuggled bush meat into the country from Africa for many years." Rat meat, apparently, is valuable enough in England to risk a prison sentence for its sale.

Historically, the world's most prolific consumers of rat meat have been the people of the Philippines. Although it's a traditional dish that's apparently been popular for centuries, disdain from Westerners like those from Spain and the U.S. (countries which occupied the island nation in the 19th and 20th centuries) has largely driven it underground. People still eat rats, but they don't like to talk about it. Sold in supermarkets as "star" meat, rats are killed and canned in an industrialized way, which greatly decreases the chances for contamination and disease transmission and indicates that the people eating it aren't exactly starving. I asked a Filipina nanny at my sons' school if she'd ever tried star meat. She shot me a nasty and surprised look as though I had brought up a deep, dark secret and quickly said no. When I pressed her on the point, she said that eating rats was something "people out in the country do" and quickly added with obvious contempt that "they'll eat anything." When I asked for star meat at some local Filipino supermarkets, the clerks told me that I couldn't get any and one added "it's illegal over here." But they all knew what I was talking about.

In the summer of 2005, an infestation of rats and other signs of impending famine started a rat-eating trend in the Arunachal Pradesh, a mountainous northern province of India that shares a border with Tibet. The hunting was kicked off when the provincial government offered a two rupee (about 4 cents in U.S. currency) bounty paid for rattails by the provincial government. "This is a real serious problem with hundreds of rats feasting on standing crops and vegetables, and even fruits," said provincial agriculture minister Tsering Gyurme. "We are looking for help to get rid of these crop raiders." Many local people, especially children, went to work catching rats. A youngster named Tai Pagang told a local newspaper that he'd killed 280 rats in a week and was delighted that the government paid him right away.

In some Asian countries, infestations of rats are considered one of the most reliable indicators of a coming food shortage. "Such unusual signs of rats destroying food grains on a large scale are a bad omen—it signals the onset of a great famine," said Gyurme. "It is not a myth or any superstitious belief to think that bamboo flowering signals famine. It is a stark reality and the region had experienced and witnessed an outbreak of famine in the past under similar circumstances."

When local crops did begin to fail and bodies of mostly tailless rats started to pile up, it didn't take much convincing to get people to start eating them. Raw rats started appearing at markets with a pair of good-sized adults fetching 10 rupees (22 cents U.S.) and rat soup with fresh herbs and barbecued rat with cracked black peppercorns became quite popular in the area. "Rat meat is oily and very tasty," said Raso Tana, a teacher who works in Arunachal Pradesh.

When the contestants on the American TV show "Survivor" ate barbecued rats, the consensus opinion was (rather disappointingly) that they "tasted like chicken"—an all-too-frequently uttered catchall used to describe a bland taste. But like snails, frog legs, and fattened goose livers, rats are often prized delicacies in some cultures. In Vietnam, rats are traditionally eaten only at weddings, but in recent years have become an everyday menu item. In the 1990s, many Vietnamese rice farmers started augmenting their earnings by hunting snakes and civets (locally referred to as "cats") and exporting them to China, where they are popular, especially in big-city restaurants. It was a shortsighted plan. Without these predators, rat populations exploded and made a huge impact on rice crops and the populations of various types of snails, another valuable food source in Southeast Asia. In 1998, Vietnamese prime minister Phan Van Khai passed a law that effectively banned both the consumption and export of snakes or civets. While it would take years for the predators to return to numbers that could make an impact on rat populations, the resourceful farmers started killing and eating rats. Rat meat quickly became so popular that, by 2002, the Vietnamese government claimed that 110 tons a week were being harvested in Bac Lieu province alone. Since farm laborers in the region get paid about $1 for a day's work, but about 12 to 15 cents for each rat, the BBC estimated that more than 2,000 people in Bac Lieu are full-time rat catchers.

Eating rats poses the same risks as consuming any wild animal and perhaps a few more as there are more diseases communicable between rats and humans. "Poor standards of processing and cooking can result in plague transmission," said Belmain. "Even the handling of the dead bodies could result in disease transmission." That said, non-diseased rats are nutritious and not just as a source of protein and fat. With an ability to synthesize vitamin C from foods humans can't, the consumption of rat meat could have warded off scurvy for sailors in the age of exploration—had they only known to eat them. Of course, sailors did eat rats—which were omnipresent—from time to time when food stocks got low. When Ferdinand Magellan, the legendary Portuguese naviga-tor, tried to circumnavigate the earth (the voyage succeeded, but he didn't—he was killed in the Philippines), stores ran

out long before the mission ended, and rats became a staple.
One of his crewmen wrote:

> We ate only old biscuit reduced to powder, and full of
> grubs, and stinking from the dirt which the rats had
> made on it when eating the good biscuit, and we drank
> water that was yellow and stinking. The men were so
> hungry that if any of them caught a rat, he could sell it
> for a high price to someone who would eat it.

An uncertain number of rats give their lives for less noble
human pursuits than science, dining, or the use of their fur
for the fine paintbrushes prized by some Japanese artists. Rat
hunting has always been a moderately popular pastime
among youngsters, especially in rural areas. It's not hard to
imagine a kid trying out his new BB gun on rats congregated
around the town dump or the family compost pile. Many people who would never kill a bird or chipmunk have little
problem shooting a rat.

If the stories traded on Web sites like Ratkill.com and
"Kurt, The Fall City Rat Hunter" are any indication, the sport
of rat hunting isn't limited to kids. One of my favorites, sub-
mitted by a fellow who calls himself "KurtS," tells the story of
a man who tired of seeing rats lick the peanut butter off his
snap traps, so he decided to go hunting. Packing a BB pistol
powerful enough to "shoot through the metal of a galvanized
garbage can," KurtS managed to pump five pellets into the
head and chest of the rodent after it jumped towards him.
When he climbed down from his sniping position on top of
the family clothes dryer to inspect his kill, he was shocked
when the rat sprung to life and leapt on top of the dryer. It

took seven more slugs (all hits) to finally bring the beast down. Brown rats, clearly, are not easy to kill.

Enthusiasts from all over the world swap stories on these sites and others about killing rats with high-powered handguns, rifles, homemade napalm, antifreeze, various types of traps, cats and dogs. The stories are exciting, dramatic and usually told in a triumphant tone. According to Ratkill.com's own poll, 24 percent of respondents say they feel "orgasmic" after killing a rat.

People either love or hate rats; I've yet to meet anyone in the middle. But even the most ardent rat-lover points out that their affection is limited to pet rats. Wild ones may get some sympathy, but very few actual advocates. I've seen firsthand many indications of how people feel about rats. The most illustrative happened in 1999, when I read a story in the *New York Times* about a pair of red-tailed hawks that were nesting in the southeast corner of Central Park. Hawks and falcons are actually pretty common in the city, but this was the first nest in the park that anyone could remember and its owners were not only very photogenic, but they had a flair for the dramatic. They were often seen resting, preening, or watching for prey while perched on the balconies of luxurious Fifth Avenue apartments owned by people like Woody Allen and Mary Tyler Moore. After work that day I went to the nesting site. There was a crowd of people around, many with cameras, binoculars, or telescopes. The female, later known as Lola, had just brought an eastern gray squirrel to the nest and was tearing it into bite-sized pieces for her young. Some of the families around were complaining about what a "gross" display it was as the serious bird people were muttering to each other about this and that. The next morning, a Saturday,

I went back and the crowd was much larger, maybe two hundred people in all. There were some oohs and aahs as the male (later named Pale Male and celebrated as a role model for fathers everywhere in newspapers, on television, and in Marie Winn's delightful book *Red Tails in Love*) circled obliviously over the crowd. Suddenly, he dropped out of the air so quickly, it looked like he had been shot. When he emerged from the trees with a live rat in his talons, its naked tail wriggling pointlessly, the crowd exploded. Those who had been seated rose to their feet in Pale Male's honor. The cheering was so loud it actually drowned out the rush of Fifth Avenue traffic. Nobody applauded the death of the squirrel.

Plague Bomb

The Japanese used the plague against enemy forces in World War II. Under the command of Lieutentant-General Shiro Ishii, the notorious Unit 731 experimented on Chinese, Korean and Western prisoners and civilians, all of whom were referred to as "dead wood." Among other atrocities, subjects were injected with plague, smallpox, cholera and botulism. Though all proved effective killers, the commanders of Unit 731 decided that plague would cause the most hysteria if unleashed. Ceramic "flea bombs" and other pathogen delivery systems were used against Chinese civilians far from occupying forces. When Ishii was foiled in his desire to use biological weapons against the Americans in the Pacific, he ordered Unit 731 disbanded and its facilities destroyed. After the war, the commanders of Unit 731 avoided serious war crimes prosecution by supplying U.S. and Soviet officials with data acquired through human experimentation.

Sources: Unit 731 Testimony by Hal Gold and Unit 731: Japan's Secret Biological Warfare in World War II by Peter Williams

Vermin,
Villain, and
God's Best Friend

T he worst thing in the world happens to be rats." Or so said O'Brien, the torturer in George Orwell's novel *1984*. In what is auguably the most memorable scene in perhaps the most significant novel of the 20th century, Orwell's hero, Winston Smith, has his spirit broken by being threatened with a box of carnivorous rats. When O'Brien begins to put the box over Smith's head, he cracks, his spirit is broken and the totalitarian Big Brother has won. Simply the thought of having the flesh on his face eaten by rats managed to force Smith to betray his lover and all of his principles.

It's a powerful scene, and one of many mentions of rats by Orwell in his work. He certainly knew what he was talking about. Orwell spent much of his adult life in abject poverty,

even homelessness—a period he chronicled well in the auto-
biographical accounts in his book *Down and Out in Paris and
London*. When he did work in those days, it was usually in
hotels or restaurants, both of which he described as teeming
with sometimes quite bold rats.

Rat expert S. Anthony Barrett, in his book *The Story of
Rats: Their Impact on Us and Our Impact on Them*, maintains
that Orwell was letting his imagination get away from him.
Writing "this hideous fantasy has no connection with what
they would actually do (they would probably be terrified),"
Barrett states that the rats would not have attacked Smith's
face, even though the scientist himself has been bitten many
times, even once contracting leptospirosis and nearly dying.
Truth is, although they could hardly be described as thirsting
for human blood, even the most docile rats will bite, often in
what appear to be unprovoked circumstances. In fact, Barrett
might be surprised to learn that incoming biology students at
the Georgia College & State University are warned: "If you
work long enough with rats, you will receive a bite."

Of course, wild rats are far more aggressive towards
humans than are lab rats or pet rats, which have been inbred
over thousands of generations to promote (but clearly not
guarantee) docility. The process could be easily reversed, by
breeding more aggressive rats with each other. And, while
1984 is certainly a work of fiction, the rat torture has some
basis in reality. During the early days of the Spanish
Inquisition (1480–1858), one of the most commonly used tor-
tures was called Trial by Rodent. The victim would be
strapped to a table and a rat would be placed on his or her
abdomen. A bronze pan would be placed over the rat and
heated with coals. The terrified rodent, hoping to escape the

searing metal, was forced to burrow through the victim's body. It's been said that the practice originated in China.

More recently, rats have been used as a mild torture in front of millions. On the NBC reality show "Fear Factor," contestants are rewarded for enduring acts most people would consider disgusting. Many of the highest-rated episodes have involved rats. Contestants have had to pick dead rats up with their mouths and spit them into garbage cans, while others have had to sort dozens of rats by sex—usually by picking them up by their tails. Particularly compelling was the episode that aired on February 9, 2004, in which a woman was made to lie in a box and was covered by dozens of rats and raw chicken legs (covering with rats had been used before, but this was the first time food was added) and her husband was required to pick out all the chicken.

All of these episodes met with protests from pro-rat organizations (especially Debbie Dumcommun's Rat Fan Club), but it wasn't until January 2005 that legal action took place. Oddly, it was a viewer with no connection to rats who filed suit. According to the claim he filed, a 49-year-old paralegal from Cleveland named Austin Aitken was watching "Fear Factor" when the contestants were obliged to drink a slurry of dead rats pureed in a blender. The sight sickened him so much that he thought NBC owed him $2.5 million. In his statement, Aitken claimed: "To have the individuals on the show eat and drink dead rats was crazy and from a viewer's point of view made me throw-up." Not only did he vomit, but Aitken claimed his blood pressure rose so high that he became him dizzy and light-headed—and then he bumped his head while running out of the room. Aitken was a regular viewer of the show and apparently didn't have any

problem when contestants ate live insects and other inverte-
brates. Perhaps he wasn't watching CBS's even more popular
reality show "Survivor" two years earlier in which contestants
hunted, cooked, and ate rats as part of their trial. On March
15, 2005, Ohio superior court judge Lesley Wells dismissed
Aitken's suit as "frivolous" and gave him a stern warning
against appealing. NBC should have thanked Aitken for the
publicity. "Fear Factor" has become even more successful and
you can now buy an official "Fear Factor" T-shirt from the network's online store that features a man about to eat a rat and
the slogan "Face Your Fears."

More often than actual perpetrators or victims of any
violent acts, rats in Western literature are often used as
creepy witnesses to outrages (as in Edgar Allan Poe's "The
Pit and the Pendulum") or as part of the scenery, a shorthand
device to connote filth (as in James Clavell's *King Rat*), contagion, tension or terror (as in Jane Austen's *Northanger
Abbey*). In the hugely popular three-film series, archaeolo-
gist-adventurer Indiana Jones is frequently harried or
chased by swarms of rats. For *Indiana Jones and the Final
Crusade*, director Steven Spielberg supervised the breeding
of two thousand rats to ensure that they were free of diseases. Producers even managed to get an insurance
policy—with a thousand-rat deductible—covering them.
Despite those precautions, the actors were often unwilling to
work with rats and more than a thousand puppet and
mechanical rats were built for the film. No matter what they
did, it wasn't enough for actress Amanda Redman, who was
slated to play the female lead, Dr. Elsa Schneider, but simply
could not overcome her fear of rats. The role instead went to
lesser-known Alison Doody.

In the story they are perhaps best known for, rats play a supporting role. The legend of the Pied Piper of Hamelin is an often-told fable which has many hundreds of variations. But the basic story is that a mayor engaged a charismatic stranger to remove a surplus of rats from his town. The medieval pest control officer did the job, charming the rats with a combination of his brilliantly spangled costume ("pied" is a somewhat archaic term meaning colorfully striped or spotted) and the music he played ("piper"). With this cunning strategy, he led every single rat out of the town. But when he returned for his reward, the piper was in for a surprise. The mayor, satisfied that the rats were gone and weren't coming back, refused to pay the piper. Some tellings of the fable go further and say that the mayor taunted and challenged the piper, certain that he was powerless. Enraged, the piper got his revenge by charming Hamelin's children the same way he had enchanted the rats and leading them out of town.

What happens next depends on the story's teller, but (as is the case in many German fables) the town's children usually wind up dead. Noted historian William Manchester found some evidence to believe the story is based in fact, writing:

> The Pied Piper of Hamelin was a real man, but there was nothing enchanting about him. Quite the

Picky Eaters

Wild rats' least-favorite foods

Raw beets
Peaches
Celery
Cooked cauliflower
Grapefruit
Raw cauliflower
Raw potatoes
Raw carrots
Raw bell peppers
Raw cabbage
Radishes
Cooked spinach
Plums
Cooked cabbage
Apples

Source: "A Preliminary Analysis of Garbage as Food for the Norway Rat," Martin W. Schein

opposite; he was horrible, a psychopath and pederast who, on June 24, 1484, spirited away 130 children in the Saxon village of Hammel and used them in unspeakable ways. Accounts of the aftermath vary. According to some, the victims were never seen again; others told of disembodied little bodies found scattered in the forest underbrush or festooning the branches of trees.

Other modern experts disagree, saying that the story goes back even further, into the latter part of the 13th century. Many discount the rats entirely, saying that the Pied Piper was simply a charismatic leader who lured the town's children to work and live in other communities, while others maintain that the whole story is a metaphor and perhaps a balm for the guilt-ridden parents who allowed their children to participate in the disastrous Children's Crusade of the early 13th century.

Rats did eventually get a starring role and underwent a period as Hollywood's most frightening animal villain in the early 1970s, until Spielberg's 1975 gothic horror classic *Jaws* made everybody terrified of going into the water. Based on Gilbert Ralston's 1969 novel *The Ratcatcher's Diary*, *Willard* is the story of a young social misfit who suffers constant indignities and retreats from human contact after he befriends two rats, Ben and Socrates. They recruit hundreds more rats who begin to obediently serve Willard through his faithful lieutenants Ben and Socrates. After Socrates is killed, Ben takes control of the swarming herd and they turn murderous, eventually devouring Willard himself. *Willard* may have tapped into a long-suppressed fear of rats (it may also have been Bruce Davison's powerful and sympathetic performance in the title role, although critic Roger Ebert maintains that "people had been waiting a long time to see Ernest Borgnine eaten alive by rats and weren't about to miss the opportunity"), but the film was an unqualified success. A sequel called *Ben*, in which the charismatic rat recruits his own boy, was made the following year. Although it did fairly well at the box office, it lacked *Willard's* subtlety and was not a critical success. It is probably best remembered for its theme song, a tender ballad sung by Michael Jackson. It was probably the first top 10 hit about a boy's love for his rat. *Willard* was remade in 2003, with self-described eccentric and rat enthusiast Crispin Glover in the title role, but, despite some positive reviews, the film drew small audiences.

When rats are anthropomorphized, their characters are usually notorious, conniving, untrustworthy, and occasionally violent—quite in contrast to mice, who are often sympathetic characters and are the animal equivalent to Everyman. One famous rat, Templeton of E. B. White's children's classic *Charlotte's Web*, is a glutton who only reluctantly helps the story's heroes after he's offered untold wealth in garbage. Exceptions have occurred, like the 1982 animated film *The Secret of NIMH*, in which a field mouse is aided by super-intelligent rats that had escaped from a laboratory. Even so, the rats do come up with a devious scheme to assassinate their own leader.

In the English language, "rat" is a word that rarely carries any positive connotation. Merriam-Webster defines rat as "a contemptible person," particularly "one who betrays or deserts friends or associates." There is a perhaps apocryphal story that takes place at Harry S. Truman's first birthday party after he became president of the United States following the death of Franklin D. Roosevelt. Just as Truman was about to blow out the candles on his cake, a rat ran across the room. As the story goes, when Truman's daughter Margaret saw the offending rodent, she screamed: "A Republican!"

Less derisive is the commonly used suffix "rat"—as in mallrat or gymrat—to describe a person who habituates a particular place, perhaps too often. And, depending on what part of the U.K. you're in, you may hear the genitalia of either sex referred to as a "rat."

More recently, the rat has been used as a metaphor by striking workers. At strikes around the United States, giant inflatable rats, some up to 30 feet tall, act as attention getters and symbols of unfair practices. In union parlance a "rat" is a non-union contractor (non-union workers are called "scabs," but it would be hard to make a recognizable balloon out of one) and the inflatable rodent with snaggly teeth, sinister claws, and an evil look on his face is used to identify them to passersby. It works. The first time I ran into a giant inflatable rat was in New York when the cleaning staff of a hotel was striking. An immense rat in front of a hotel is a pretty strong image. I was one of perhaps two dozen people who were milling around asking questions about it. "The rat gets people to stop and ask questions about what's going on," said Jerry Kraft, president of Local 79 Construction and General Building Laborers in Manhattan. "That's why we use it."

They might not get to for very long. The use of the rat has been challenged and will appear before the Supreme Court of the United States. "I would like to see this get decided by the Supreme Court because there are many employers that are impacted by this conduct," said Kathryn Davis, a San Francisco lawyer who frequently deals with labor issues. "Particularly now as the unions step up their recruitment drives and attempts to reinforce membership, we are going to see more of it (use of rat balloons)." The problem is that the rat has been defined in some courts as picketing, as it has the potential to intimidate people into not dealing with the targeted business. And, in most jurisdictions, picketing is only allowed during strikes. Even if the court rules against it, the rat wouldn't be exterminated, as it could still be used in actual strike situations. Lowell Peterson, a New York–based lawyer who often represents unions, said that other animal balloons could be used by organized labor if the rat is struck down. "There are plenty of other animals," he said. So far, skunk and cockroach balloons have been floated, but none carries the impact of the rat.

Cultural enmity for rats is not universal. Traditional Chinese beliefs consider rats as a symbol of good luck and wealth. Some stories maintain that humans actually owe rats a considerable debt as the rodents introduced them to rice, an invaluable discovery. In the fable that became the basis of the Chinese zodiac, the rat is one of twelve animals which must report to the Jade Emperor. Each animal was to be rewarded by how quickly it arrived, so there was great competition among them. The rat—generally characterized as charming, witty, and self-effacing, but somewhat devious—forgot to tell his good friend the cat about the race, ensuring the beginnings of a hatred between the two. Eventually, the animals have to cross a lake to get to the Jade Emperor. In what appears to be an act of contrition, the rat suggests to the cat that they ride together on the back of the ox (most likely a water buffalo) because he was the strongest swimmer. The cat accepts and, just as they are about to get to the other side, the rat pushes the cat into the water. The rat leapt from the ox and finished first, receiving the honor of having the first year of the twelve-year Chinese astrological cycle named after him. The unfortunate cat arrived thirteenth, too late to be included in the zodiac, and bitterly swore revenge.

People born in the year of the rat are reputed to have great degrees of charm, intelligence, passion, elegance, generosity to family and friends, opportunism, and honesty. The yin to that yang can include greed, hoarding, a personal coldness, and a tendency to overwork, often at the expense of family and friends. Those born under the rat sign are said to be even-tempered, but can be vicious if provoked.

The rat also occupies a similarly enviable spot in Hindu mythology. Ganesh (also know as Ganesha, Ganesa, Vinayaka, Vinayagar, and other variations on his 108 official names) is a four-armed man with a potbelly and an elephant's head. One of the most prominent and beloved deities in Hinduism, Ganesh is recognized as the lord of wisdom, intelligence, prudence, education, good luck, gates and doors, houses and literature. He is probably best known as the remover of obstacles, which has made it customary for Hindus to invoke Ganesh before the undertaking of any major task. Frequently, businesses owned by Hindus will have a small shrine to Ganesh—Apu Nahasapeemapetilon, a Hindu, has one at his Kwik-E-Mart convenience store on "The Simpsons."

Virtually every depiction of Ganesh also contains the likeness of a rat. Like other Hindu deities, Ganesh travels on a *vahana*, an animal that acts as vehicle (actually carrying the master), servant and, in the case of Ganesh and his rat, friends. Ganesh's *vahana* is Mooshika, a small and pious rat (sometimes referred to as a mouse) with enormous strength.

Mooshika serves as a humble counterpoint to Ganesh's greatness. While both enjoy sweets, Mooshika never fails to give thanks and pray before eating—something Ganesh doesn't always see a need to do. Conversely, Mooshika is known for his inability to rein in his fickle desires, but a few gentle whacks from Ganesh's goad are usually enough to keep him in line. There is a specific shloka (32-syllable verses that make up most of Sanskrit holy texts, many of which are still chanted by devout Hindus) to honor Ganesh that mentions Mooshika:

Mooshika vaahana modhaha hastha
Chamara karna vilambitha suthra
Vamana rupa maheswara puthra
Vigna vinayaga padha namaste

Loosely translated, the shloka says:

He who has the rat named Mooshika as his vahana, He who always keeps modhaham [a coconut and rice sweet favored by both Ganesh and Mooshika]. He who has ears that look like a fan, He who wears a chain-like belt around his waist, He who is short of stature, He who is the son of Lord Parameshwara. O! Lord Vinayaka who is all the above and he who always annuls all impediments, We worship your Divine Feet.

While Mooshika is no god, he does have one for a best friend.

But there is a place in India where rats are treated with almost god-like reverence. Near the town of Deshnok in the Thar Desert in the northwest part of the country, there's a popular tourist spot called the Karnimata temple. As you approach it, you can see long lines of people, some carrying coconuts, others carrying bread. Dedicated to a 15th century mystic named Karnimata, whom many believed was a human incarnation of the Hindu deity Durga, the temple is a holy shrine for local Hindus. The temple itself is ornate in typical Hindu style, with marble columns and lots of intricate reliefs. Red banners are strewn over the facade and wire mesh is mounted in the open areas of the courtyard to keep the massed forces of pigeons outside of the temple.

Getting closer, one notices that the exterior of the temple is covered with images of Karnimata, lions and thousands and thousands of rats. It's a fairly attractive sight until many of the images begin to move. As is typical of Hindu tradition, visitors must remove their shoes and socks before they can enter, but many tourists later wish they hadn't. Once they enter the temple, visitors are exposed to about twenty thousand rats (some estimates run as high as three hundred thousand, but people traditionally love to inflate the numbers of rats) and a wall-to-wall carpet of their droppings. Rats pour out of holes in the wall in unending streams, they congregate under furniture, they swarm over bowls of food and milk left out for them, they crawl over the faithful and they skitter along the floor in every direction. It's said to be a sign of particular good fortune if a rat strides over a visitor's foot, and that charm in increased dramatically if it was one of the temple's two white rats. Many people feed the rats by hand, which is itself considered a blessing, and there is some competition to see who gets to finish any food nibbled and left unfinished by the rats, as sharing a meal with them is considered to be a high honor. It's an unsettling sight when four or more people wrestle in a pile of rat feces for the right to eat a shard of coconut that has been left behind by an overfed rat.

Rats became sacred in the area when Karnimata's step-son Laxman drowned in a tank he was attempting to drink from. Karnimata implored Yama, the god of death, to restore his life. Yama refused, then relented and permitted Laxman and all of Karnimata's male children to come into the world as rats. Consequently, many Hindu faithful in the area con-sider the rats to be direct descendants of Durga and, therefore, quite holy. Only rats within the temple complex are treated in this way, not as rats but as reincarnated holy peo-ple. While the majority of Hindus seem to consider the people who honor Karnimata in this way (also known as Charans) a bit of a naive cult, the temple is respectfully pro-tected and, when pneumonic plague broke out in India in 1994, government extermination programs did not target the Karnimata rats.

Although nobody has yet to complain about being disap-pointed by the number of rats (or the unholy smell), many Western visitors are surprised by how small the Karnimata rats are. "I have rats at home," a clearly disappointed Australian tourist told the BBC. "And these guys are more like mice." The rats at Karnimata, like most in India, are *Rattus rattus*, rather than the *Rattus norvegicus* most often encoun-tered in more temperate climates. Since the residents of Karnimata are almost uniformly brown, it's hard to tell peo-ple that these are black rats, not brown rats. But clearly they are, spending as much time climbing as they do running around flat surfaces and often clinging to the chicken wire, which is officially in place to protect the rats from birds of prey. Perhaps they're trying to snag one of the thousands of resident pigeons to add a little protein to the strictly vegetarian diet provided by the Hindu faithful.

Despite the rarefied environment, some signs of typical black-rat behavior can be seen throughout the temple complex. The rats inside the building are overwhelmingly young and healthy and the more aggressively competitive ones tend to dominate the milk and food bowls. Outside the building, old, sick, and injured rats that have been driven out hang around—often showing signs of bites on their tails and hindquarters—looking for handouts and braving the native falcons.

Although the people who run the temple claim that "no diseases related to rats have been found," there is always a surplus of rather afflicted-looking people begging for alms in town, all the way up to the temple doors. The proclamation of the temple being a disease-free environment also loses some credibility when coupled with another claim the Karnimata elders make: "Neither the temple stinks of foul smells nor is it dirty anywhere." Both parts of that particular statement are far from true.

But the relationship between the rats and people of India is complex. Many people in the country eat rat meat and some use a mixture of rat embryos and water as a cure-all medicine. Even devout Hindus, who never eat meat and have deep spiritual connections to rats through Mooshika and Durga, are forced to trap them at grain silos and relocate them to a place where they believe they'll do less harm. But throughout the country, rats are tolerated and even fed by people in parks, much like squirrels and pigeons in the West. For most of the world, though, the sight of a wild rat evokes fear, revulsion, and a desire to exterminate.

"Don't Take Are Rats"

Sample from the online petition to stop the proposed ban of pet rats by the Saskatchewan government:

I have owned pet rats for over 10 years, and they are the most kind and loving rodents i have ever known. I cannot believe anyone would want to ban owning pet rats. Most times, i would prefer to have a pet rat over a dog or cat; they are just that wonderful. None of mine have ever had any illnesses that were harmful to humans, and i have never been bit seriously (I've only been bit a few times in my years of rat ownership). They are safe pets and everyone deserves the right to own them.

Source: petitiononline.com

Destroyer of Worlds

When Pete McClelland wakes up at 4 a.m., the first thing he does is check to see if the zipper on his tent has frozen shut. If it hasn't, he looks out at the cloth he tied the night before to the tail boom of the helicopter parked closest to his tent. "If it was horizontal, it meant that the wind was too strong to fly, so I could roll over and enjoy the luxury of a lie-in for an hour—with regular checks in case the wind died down and the cloth stopped waving," he said. "If it wasn't horizontal then there was a reasonable chance that it (the wind) wasn't blowing too strongly and we may be able to drop that day—so out of my pit and go outside to confirm the wind and see if it was raining, if it was looking likely, the engineer we had would crank up the generator to give us light and I would wake the rest of the team." He'd need their help—he had two hundred thousand rats to kill.

McClelland, program manager, Outlying Islands for the New Zealand Department of Conservation, is responsible for—among many other things—ridding the islands between New Zealand and Antarctica of the rats that have infested them. His job is to systematically reclaim the islands that rats had overrun to help them return to their pre-rat status. The worst affected of them was Campbell Island. A little more than 400 miles south of New Zealand's South Island, Campbell Island is not all that much farther from the Antarctic coast than it is to Wellington, the nation's capital.

Formed by ancient volcanoes, Campbell Island is surrounded by high cliffs. Above the rocks is about 43 square miles of rolling meadows covered with three or four kinds of thick, scraggly grass. The grass never gets very high because Campbell Island is constantly whipped by winds, often strong enough to knock a man down.

Discovered by Captain Fredrick Hasselburg on January 4, 1810, he named it in honor of his employers, the Campbell Brothers seal oil company of Sydney, Australia. The island was used intermittently for the next few decades as a sealing and whaling station until overhunting depleted their stocks.

Other than proximity to marine mammals, there wasn't much reason to go to Campbell Island. "The land had a sad aspect," said cartographer Bouquet de la Grye of the French Hydrographic Office, when he visited in 1874. "Everything was gray on the land, gray in the sky and gray on the sea."

In 1896, an ambitious Scottish immigrant named James Gordon took out a lease on the island, intending to raise sheep. He failed almost immediately. In 1900, his venture was bought out by another recent immigrant from Britain, Captain Henry Tucker, who brought 1100 tough merino sheep to the island.

Although the sheep didn't seem to mind the weather and the isolation, the shepherds he hired did and Tucker had a hard time keeping staff on the island. He finally resorted to importing high-priced shepherds from the Shetland Islands off Scotland, who he decided had suitably tough dispositions after he met them. Tucker's plan might have worked, but he didn't account for the fact that Antarctic grasses grow extremely slowly. The sheep population, which peaked at about eight thousand in 1913, ate everything green on the island and began to starve when it didn't grow back right away.

As the value of the wool raised on the island fell below the price of hiring a ship to go get it, Tucker abandoned the plan and the shepherds were eventually rescued by a government boat on a mapping mission two years after the last wool boat had left. Tucker's lease was bought in 1927 at an auction by a farmer named John Warren, who brought five thousand more sheep to the island and even tried to live there himself. In 1931, Warren and his employees—starving—were rescued from the island and it eventually was set aside as a nature preserve. The sheep mostly starved to death and, starting in 1970, the New Zealand government would periodically send teams of men to the island to kill the remainder. The last was shot in 1992.

A single rusted stove and a few wires from long-forgotten fences are all that remain of the humans who tried repeatedly to take over the island. The rest of what they brought either starved, rotted, or blew away. Except the rats.

Starting with Captain Hasselburg, pretty well every ship that visited Campbell Island brought with it a healthy complement of robust brown rats (black rats were already pretty rare around New Zealand, even on shipping, by 1810). Unaffected by the winds and enjoying a climate that not often fell very far below freezing and that never got too hot, the rats quickly dug homes and stamped down runs in the grass. And there was always plenty to eat. As first, the rats probably fed on the discarded portions of the seal and whale carcasses and, later, most likely got fat on the young, sick and dying, helpless sheep trapped on the island.

But even without these gifts from careless humans, rats had no problem staying well fed on Campbell Island. Like most bits of land in the ocean—particularly those around Antarctica—Campbell Island is the breeding ground for many different types of marine mammals and birds. With no native land predators, the inhabitants never developed much in the way of self-defense. Many of the birds native to islands like Campbell flew poorly if at all and none made any effort to hide, protect, or defend their nests. Rats feasted on eggs and hatchlings and even the occasional baby seal. As the numbers of rats rose, the population of native species plum- meted. "The rats killed all the native land birds and smaller seabirds on Campbell—most of them before they were even discovered by science," said McClelland. "They included a flightless teal that had just two specimens collected on the coast before being discovered on a small offshore island in 1976, an endemic snipe that was only discovered in 1997 on an inaccessible (42-acre) island and a parakeet that is only known from one bone collected in 2004."

Unlike the sheep, when the rats' preferred food sources became scarce (the birds were practically wiped out by 1840) they simply changed their diet. "They will eat almost any- thing—animal or vegetable," said McClelland. "Eggs, chicks, small ground and sea birds, seeds, seedlings, lizards, inverte- brates—they will eat intertidal shellfish and even dive for them along with fresh water crayfish and basically anything else they can catch—it's all on the menu for a hungry rat." The rats even ate the wallpaper paste from the island's few buildings before the structures eventually collapsed and were blown away. While Campbell Island may have proven too tough a place for sheep or humans, it suited the rats fine. By 2000, more than two hundred thousand of them lived on the little island, giving it the dubious distinction of being the most densely rat-infested place on earth.

Eager to reclaim the island on behalf of the birds and marine mammals who originally called it home, in June 2001, the New Zealand Department of Conservation gave McClelland nineteen people, two ships, five helicopters, 140 tons of rat poison, and a directive to rid Campbell Island of rats once and for all. Planning the operation like a military assault, McClelland knew he had to hurry. The only way he could get the rats to eat the poison was to drop it in winter when other food sources were scarce. Bereft of contact with humans or any other predators for generations, the rats of Campbell Island were probably the least suspicious in the world. But no matter how naive they were, McClelland knew it's easier to poison a hungry rat than a fat one. He was also smart enough to use brodifacoum, a second-generation anti-coagulant that causes rats to bleed to death through their digestive system. Quickly degraded in normal environmental conditions, the poison is generally considered most danger-ous to non-target species when they eat rats who have ingested it. Since the rats on Campbell had no predators, the potential for accidental deaths was minimal.

After two years of freezing in tents, directing helicopter traffic, and dropping ton after ton of poison pellets on to one of the most remote and unforgiving places in the world, McClelland and his team brought in a specially trained pack of dogs to track down any survivors. The government of New Zealand officially declared Campbell Island rat free in May 2003. The whole country celebrated. "A team of conservation officers returned from Campbell Island today with the news that after months of surveying and trapping, they have been unable to find any trace of rats whatsoever," announced Conservation Minister Chris Carter. "This is a fantastic result. It is a proud day for New Zealand conservation and proves once again that we are the world leaders in pest control and protection of our native species."

Since then, Campbell Island has begun to return to its pre-rat state with surprising quickness. "The vegetation recovery, along with all the animal life, is truly amazing," said McClelland. "There are carpets of seedlings where previously very few survived." Even more amazing is the recovery of the Campbell Island teal, a small flightless duck that was thought to be extinct after none had been sighted since 1944. But in 1976, a park ranger named Rodney Russ was on Dent Island—a lonely piece of rock the size of a suburban strip mall about 2 miles from Campbell Island—when he saw something brown move in the grass. He was sure that rats had finally invaded what many considered the last rat-free piece of land in the South Pacific and was determined to do his part to stop them. He made a diving, gloveless grab and was surprised when he came up with a duck. Later that day, he caught another.

These two specimens—who biologists determined lived off the excrement and regurgitations of passing gulls—appeared to be all that was left of the species. Both were female, but the one Russ caught first (later named Daisy the Duck) was pregnant. She was taken to Mount Bruce nature center where, under constant supervision and protection, she eventually gave birth to a number of litters—twenty-four ducklings in all. In 1984, a scientific team found three more females and one male (Swampy) on Dent Island and added them to the breeding stock. Although McClelland still harbored some fears that the rats weren't entirely eradicated ("never underestimate a rat" has become his personal motto), he was eager to return the teals to the wild. "There was a risk they'd turn into cage birds," he said. "They were living the life of Riley up at Mount Bruce. We actually had to slim them down before we brought them back to Campbell. Take a couch potato and run it in a marathon and it's not going to last too well." In October 2005, McClelland was given the honor of lifting the door on the little wooden box that contained the first Campbell Island teals to be returned to their natural, rat-free home. With a total population of about 180, the Campbell Island teal has since been upgraded from "critically endangered" to "threatened."

Campbell Island isn't the first piece of land to be freed of rats, just the most well known. McClelland and his team started with some smaller islands first and the U.S. Fish and Wildlife Service exterminated the rats, pigs, and other invasive species on tiny Laysan Island in the Hawaiian Archipelago (thereby saving the endangered Laysan teal and other species) in 1967.

Though certainly admirable and encouraging, the work of McClelland and people like him is a very tiny drop in an ocean of rat infestation. Because of a habit of following humans and their food onto ships, rats have gone everywhere we have been. And, in most cases, some stay behind. Because of the rat's excellent swimming ability, they can colonize places humans have not set foot on and they can survive ship-wrecks that leave no humans alive. And, as I have been repeatedly told by scientists and exterminators alike, "It only takes one pregnant rat to start an infestation."

Although rats can thrive virtually anywhere, they do par-ticularly well on islands, especially small ones. Islands generally have few if any land-based predators and are rarely visited by birds of prey capable of taking down rats. Without any predators, rats can reproduce to populations as large as their food supply will allow. Since rats are such opportunistic feeders, food can be pretty much anything living or dead. That is of particular concern on islands where many, some-times unique species of animals and plants have evolved without the ability to hide or defend themselves from preda-tors, especially determined rats. Although it has happened in places as diverse as the freezing Aleutians west of Alaska, sunny Guadalupe in the Caribbean, moist New Caledonia north of Australia, and windswept South Georgia in the South Atlantic, the stories are amazingly similar. Soon after humans arrive at an island, rats settle there and start extermi-nating the local wildlife.

Rat migration was slow until Europeans started sailing and rats tagged along. Rats occupied ships, eating from the stores and living virtually anywhere in their holds, cabins, or even the wooden structures themselves. When the ships landed, their rats—usually with a few new litters in their numbers—landed with them. Often desperate for fresh food and water after their long trip, ship rats were among the first sailors to embark and colonize new territory.

Their own exploration began in earnest when the Portuguese began sailing outside their familiar waters. An almost rectangular country surrounded on two sides by water and two sides by constantly warring Spain, Portugal turned to the sea for trading wealth. The Portuguese first projected their force in 1415 by conquering the Moroccan port city of Ceuta (still a European enclave despite being on the continent of Africa).

Intent on finding a safer and faster path to the rich kingdoms of India and China, navigators like Bartholomeu Dias and Vasco da Gama sailed around the Cape of Good Hope (the southernmost tip of Africa) and became the first Europeans to enter the Indian Ocean. Da Gama finally reached India in 1498, establishing a trading post at what is now the modern city of Goa. Before long, the Portuguese enjoyed almost unchallenged seaborne trading routes to Asia and the Americas after Pedro Alvares Cabral got lost in a storm in 1502 and landed in Brazil. Although the Portuguese empire faded as more powerful European countries took to the seas, there are still thousands of forts, churches, towns, and families all over Africa, Asia, and the Americas bearing Portuguese names.

At first, the Portuguese sailors did their best to stay within sight of the coast, but they eventually got bolder and trusted their ships to take them over great stretches of open water. In 1505, a navigator named Domingo Fernandez Pereira was sailing from Mozambique to India when he passed by Mauritius, a large island about 700 miles east of Madagascar. He didn't stop, but he did name it Ilha do Cerne (Island of Swans). Two years later, a sailor named Pero Mascarenhas explored the group of islands including Mauritius, Réunion, and Rodrigues, and named them the

Mascarenes after himself. When his crew rowed up to the beach, they came into contact with what Pereira told the people back home were swans.

Even from a distance, it was quite a stretch to call these birds swans. Large (up to 50 pounds), gray and flightless, the odd-looking birds had outsized curved beaks and naked faces that the sailors considered comical. After evolving on an island with no predators, the birds had no fear of humans and quickly gathered to investigate the group of new animals that had arrived on their beach. The Portuguese mistook the birds' inquisitiveness for stupidity and named the birds "doudo" (their word for simpleton, it still exists in modern Portuguese as "doido," meaning foolish or insane). The sailors found the birds ridiculously simple to kill, but horribly greasy and unpalatable. Although it has frequently been written that sailors regularly hunted the dodo for food, there's no evidence that people ate them except under the most dire of circumstances.

The Portuguese never settled the islands, using them mostly just as a landmark and occasional resting point on their way to India from Africa. As their empire waned, the Dutch took over many of their trading routes, and in 1598, a sailor named Wybrant Warwijck landed on Ilha do Cerne and changed its named to Mauritius to honor his sponsor, Prince Maurits I of the Netherlands. Warwijck surveyed the island and reported that it was rich in ebony. He also mentioned the dodo, a few pigs and goats the Portuguese had left behind in an effort to establish a ready food supply and become feral— and an infestation of rats.

The Dutch used Mauritius in much the same way the Portuguese had until fear of French and British encroachment forced them to build Fort Frederik Hendrik in 1638. The twenty-five Dutchmen stationed there were the first humans ever to live on Mauritius, and they didn't eat dodos. Archaeological digs in and around the fort have revealed no dodo remains there and the Dutch called the dodo an even more insulting name than the Portuguese had—"walgvogel," which can only be translated as "disgusting bird."

Even if they had liked the taste of dodos, the Dutch would have had a hard time finding any, as the birds were already extremely rare by the time they arrived. Only one dodo was sighted in 1638 and the next one was spotted in 1662 after the fort had been abandoned. Volkert Evertsz, a Dutchman who was shipwrecked on the otherwise unpopulated island, caught a glimpse of a single specimen. Although desperate for food, he made no attempt to catch or eat the bird. The Dutch eventually came back and tried to grow sugarcane on Mauritius. Modern scientists (led by Julian Hume of the British Natural History Museum) have analyzed the hunting diaries of one of the more prominent farmers, Isaac Joan Lamotius, and have determined that the dodo probably lingered on unseen by humans until it finally disappeared altogether in 1693.

All that remains of the dodo now are a single skeleton and a poorly preserved head. Although the feral pigs may have taken a few and the humans' feeble attempts at farming probably ruined some habitat, it's widely accepted that invasive black rats are responsible for the dodo's demise by eating its unprotected eggs and chicks.

Although the dodo's story is the best known of its type and has become synonymous with careless extinction, it's hardly unique. On Mauritius alone, rats have been responsible for the extinction of at least twelve known species of birds, along with lizards, snails, plants and perhaps many others never seen by humans. On other islands, countless species have been exterminated by invasive rats and many have been brought to the brink of extinction. Notably, invasive brown or black rats have often caused the extinction of endemic rats (such as the Hispanolan spiny rat and the Cuban rice rat) and have brought others (like the Enggano rat and Sulawesi bear rat) to critical levels of endangerment. According to the U.S. Department of Agriculture, invasive species are the second leading cause of wild animal and plant endangerment and extinction, following closely behind the catchall category of habitat loss. Of the top thousand most endangered species listed as endangered by the Nature Conservancy, 42 percent are at risk from invasive species, usually rats. According to the United Kingdom Overseas Territories Conservation Forum, an umbrella group of island environmental organizations, invasive species (not including humans) have been the primary cause of 39 percent of all animal extinctions since 1600.

Darren Christie, Island Restoration Officer for the Falkland Islands, may have an even bigger job than McClelland's. There's not that much to the Falklands, really, just more windswept subantarctic rocks with little more than hauling-in beaches for seals, deafening colonies of seabirds stinking of guano, and people who spend their time fishing or tending sheep. Although the maps shown on television and in newspapers during the 1982 Falklands war made them look like two islands, it is actually an archipelago of almost eight hundred pieces of land.

Discovered in 1600 by a Dutch sailor named Sebald de Weert, the uninhabited rocks were taken over by the British in

1690 and named them after Anthony Cary, the Viscount of Falkland and the man who financed the expedition. The French landed in 1764 and promptly set up a fort. The British responded by building their own fort on a different island in 1766. Later that year, the French sold their claim to the islands to the Spanish. When the British abandoned their fort in 1774, they left behind a bronze plaque asserting their claim and warning off intruders. The Spanish ignored it, quickly established a settlement, which they abandoned in 1811. In 1816, Argentina declared independence from Spain and laid its own claim to the islands. In 1820, they established a penal colony there but it was destroyed by the United States Navy during a dispute over fishing rights in the area. In 1833, the British evicted the few remaining Argentine prisoners and began to ship in immigrants, who have stayed ever since.

Of course, each of these discoveries, landings, garrisons, and settlements brought rats. According to Christie's best estimates, about 97 percent of the Falklands' total land area is infested with invasive rats. Of course, their presence has led to the total extermination of many species of native birds and the endangerment of others. A veteran of operations on other islands, Christie doesn't have McClelland's

As big as a cat

Size comparison between frequently confused species.

House mouse
 Length: 130–198 mm, weight: 18–23 g
Black rat
 Length: 325–455 mm, weight: 115–350 g
Brown rat
 Length: 316–460 mm, weight: 195–485 g
Opossum
 Length: 645–1017 mm, weight: 1800–6300 g
Feral house cat
 Length: 720–810 mm, weight: 3100–9900 g

Source: National Wildlife Federation

budget, but he too is spreading brodifacoum by the ton in an effort to combat the rats.

Very few people missed the dodo, but people eventually began to consider rat infestations on their islands to be a major problem. But it was economics, not ecology, that drove the first offensives against rats. Farmers began to realize that rats were eating growing proportions of their crops—perhaps after eating all of the native wildlife—and had to be stopped. With poisoning too complicated and trapping too labor-intensive, many communities imported predators which they hoped would wipe the rats out as the rats had the native animals. It never worked and often the exotic predators did almost as much damage to the local fauna as they did to the rats. Even under ideal circumstances, rats are hard to kill and when local prey is available, introduced predators will choose the easier option.

At first, cats were tried in various places, but they clearly had little interest in hunting rats because the native fauna was so much easier to catch. In 1877, sugarcane planters introduced Indian mongooses to northern Puerto Rico with disastrous effects. Although the mongoose is an excellent ratter, its introduction to Puerto Rico had no effect on the island's rat population but did lead to the rapid extinction of at least twelve different species of reptiles, amphibians, and birds. Like the cats, the rats preferred to eat the local animals, which had never faced predators before. What the people who introduced the mongooses didn't realize is that the particular type they chose doesn't have the ability to climb trees. Although they are skilled hunters, the mongooses couldn't chase the rats when they scurried up trees to escape. When stocks of local animals ran out, the mongooses still avoided the hard-to-catch rats and turned to poultry and other live-stock. Making matters worse, their bites have also spread diseases (including leptospirosis) to humans.

Similarly disheartening mongoose introductions occurred in Jamaica, Costa Rica, Hawaii, Florida, Fiji, and other places, mainly around the Caribbean. Like the old lady from the children's song "who swallowed a spider to catch the fly" she'd swallowed earlier, many tropical farmers found that the introduction of mongooses gave them two pests where they'd only had one earlier. Despite extensive efforts to erad-icate them, invasive-wildlife expert David Pimental estimates that mongooses still cost American farmers about $50 mil-lion annually in lost livestock.

Yes They Can

Rats can spread rabies. Although the disease is rare among them and rabies shots are not usually administered as part of rat bite treatment, all mammals can carry the disease. Small animals rarely transfer the disease because it kills them quickly, although reports of rodent-borne rabies are increasing. No cases of rat-to-human rabies transfer have been recorded in North America, but since 1991, it has occurred in Poland, Israel, Surinam and Thailand. Both brown and black rats have been involved. The popular idea that rats can deliver a "dry bite" free of saliva because their incisors are so far forward is a completely untrue. Rat incisors are as bathed in saliva as the rest of their teeth.

Sources: Centers for Disease Prevention and Control, National Association of State Public Health Veterinarians, World Health Organization

Second Only to Us

I 'm up to my knees in human feces, urine, and other filth. It's freezing and dark and since everything—the pipes, the bricks, the holes—look exactly alike, I'm almost completely disoriented. Every once in a while a condom or some other object that should not have been flushed down a toilet drifts by to remind me what direction we're headed. Unless you have ever been in a sewer, you can't really imagine what it smells like.

As ghastly and disgusting as it all is, it's not actually terrifying—but the rats are. But that's why I'm there. I'm in the sewer to find out how rats live. The sewer I'm in isn't exactly teeming with them, but they are plenty of them in what seems like every direction. They scurry along ledges and pop out of holes. They run over one another and occasionally punch each other, but they mostly just stare at the giants who have invaded their home. As we pass, some rats let out high-pitched chirps, which are echoed by rats farther up the pipe. I don't know what they're saying about us, but it's not good.

They don't seem afraid of us. The leader of our little group is Ang, a big man with dark curly hair who looks and acts more like Big Pussy, the character played by Vincent Pastore on "The Sopranos," than Art Carney's Ed Norton from "The Honeymooners." He's tough, serious, and seemingly fearless. He tells me that he knows "everything you'd ever want to know about rats—and more." I don't doubt him, and I ask if I can see a real sewer rat close up. He tells me to wait and I do. I hear Craig, a skinny guy with long hair and a wispy mustache who describes himself as "a partier," giggling behind me. Suddenly, Ang slams the wall with his shovel. All the rats—except for the one he hit—run, screeching warnings to each other and what are probably curses at us. Despite the traumatic blow (I'm sure it would have killed me), the rat is not dead, just stunned. Ang tells me not to get too close to it because they can bite through my thick work gloves "like they're not even there." As I approach the motionless animal, some of the guys shout "boo!"—I jump every time. When I'm about an arm's length away, the rat gets to its feet and runs away. I reel back and almost fall into the sewage. All the other humans laugh. Great, I think to myself. Not only am I lost underground with a million pissed-off rats, but I'm with a bunch of total bastards.

Almost as soon as the injured rat skittered away, the others came back. To my surprise, they weren't bent on revenge, just curious and eager to get on with their daily business. Two rush out to a ledge that has a small puddle of what appears to be rainwater. I watched as the younger-looking rat laps up the water like a dog or cat, while the other brings it up to its mouth with cupped hands. They don't appear to be afraid as I approach, but they do keep a cautious eye on me. "Don't be such a baby," Ang says when he notices how timidly I approach them. "Rats will only bite you if you try to pick them up."

He's wrong, but I'm not stupid enough to tell him that while we're underground. Although it is true that rats would prefer to run than fight and never go out intending to harm humans, they bite for various reasons. According to the medical and scientific sources I have accessed, the majority of rat bites are accidental. By nature nocturnal, rats will sometimes climb into beds with humans if they smell food on them. Most times, the rats will be content to lick any food residue off the person's face or hands, but a lapse in the rat's judgment can sometimes lead to a bite. Sadly, the most frequent victims of rat bites are babies and small children because they are heavy sleepers and are likely to have leftover food, often milk (a rat favorite), on their faces or fingers. In his book *More Cunning Than Man: A Social History of Rats and Men*, Robert Hendrickson writes: "The baby cooed and sighed. Stealthily, the rat approached the sounds and smells. Instantly, it was between the infant's folded legs smelling at the diaper: whiskers, tail, and paws scraping against skin." A tad melodramatic perhaps, but hardly fantastical.

Since the bites are accidental, little physical damage is usually done and most go unreported. Of course, since most victims are small children who are sleeping, they often have a very hard time describing what happened to them and parents may never know. Other people have reported being bitten when hand-feeding rats, getting between a rat fighting with a dog or cat, disturbing sleeping rats or reaching under a sofa or into some other dark spot without looking first. According to the World Health Organization, five people died in 2003 of rat bites in which no disease was transmitted.

In 1979, a young woman told New York newspapers that she had been attacked by a horde of rats. At the time she made the claim, the city was overwhelmed by a surfeit garbage due to a tugboat strike (Manhattan had been sailing its refuse to the enormous Fresh Kills landfill in nearby Staten Island, but when the ports closed, the garbage stayed put until the Coast Guard was ordered to start hauling it). Much of the city's refuse was placed in a giant hole downtown on Ann Street not far from City Hall where a bar had blown up nine years earlier. The scene was a horrific pile of trash that practically boiled with feasting rats, so when the woman (who was never identified) told people, and the papers, everyone believed her. The story of a horde of rats descending upon an innocent woman made front pages around the world and put a serious dent in New York City's already struggling tourist trade.

Everyone believed her, that is, except the police. When the story came out the next morning, the staff of the 1st Precinct of the New York Police Department canvassed hospitals within a 50-mile radius. Nobody was admitted that night (or even that week) for injuries consistent with a massed rat attack. That doesn't mean massed rat attacks don't happen, just that nobody has ever shown me conclusive evidence of them.

In the sewer, I can't help hoping that I'm not the first. I can't reveal which sewer I was in because wasn't actually there on an authorized visit. Despite a large number of polite entreaties, no city was willing to let me report about rats from their sewers. Most didn't even answer. I only got down this one because a friend of a friend who owed me a favor knew Ang, and he said it was okay as long as I didn't "act like an idiot." The city I'm under is not special—it's a big industrial center in the Great Lakes region that has seen better days but is blessed with an excellent sewer system that's more than 150 years old. It's one of the old-style combined sewers in which the sewage and street runoff are combined. It's cheap and usually efficient, but in times of heavy snow or snow melting, raw sewage gets carried into the lake.

Ang and his team have been together for a while and everybody seems to have fallen into their role. They're used to the rats and none of them has ever really had any problems with them. "It creeps you out at first, but what isn't creepy down here?" said Craig. "I find the cockroaches way worse—at least the rats are like animals, y'know, they act in a way you can understand."

Traditionally, sewer workers have appreciated and been comforted by the presence of rats. They serve in a role roughly analogous to that of coal-mine canaries. "When you see the rats all moving in one direction, you follow them," said Ang. "If there's something that's scared the rats, it's probably gonna scare me too."

The sewer is one of humankind's greatest innovations, and one of the primary reasons we have them is to keep rats out of our homes. Although quite complex sewers existed in the Indus Valley civilization and in ancient Rome with the Cloaca Maxima, most have a less noble heritage. Medieval European townspeople generally dug communal trenches at the sides of their roads into which human and animal waste matter were thrown along with household garbage. These fetid canals gathered all kinds of opportunistic wildlife, including mosquitoes, fleas, ticks, dogs (which generally didn't hold the prestigious spot in society they enjoy now) and, of course, rats. Eventually, the stinking troughs were covered over, giving birth not only to primitive sewers but also to sidewalks. Holes, not unlike today's sewer grates, were built periodically into the covers to allow people to pour in their refuse and to allow rain to enter, in theory sweeping the filth away to a large body of water or at least out of town.

Of course, while the health benefits of taking filth away from human habitation can't be overestimated, the sewers did provide rats with a comfortable home complete with relative warmth, fresh water, access to food and human dwellings and, perhaps most important, freedom from predators. Despite rumors to the contrary, Ang assures me there aren't any alligators in the sewers, not even in Florida (although there were in Manhattan in the 1930s, according to the *New York Times*). Better even from a rat's perspective is that our sewers closely resemble the way rats lived in the wild and prefer to live now. The constant darkness is reassuring to a nocturnal, burrowing animal and the small pipes, gutters, and ledges provide the close-in constant contact that touch-loving rats crave.

Before brown rats became so closely associated with humans, they dug elaborate burrow networks in riverbanks. Now they prefer being close to man-made structures, especially vertical walls or horizontal slabs of concrete. It's frequently reported that rats live in the walls of homes, but that's actually very rare. When rats are heard in walls, it's because they are using them as thoroughfares on their way to or from their actual nest. Typically begun by a pregnant female, rats like to dig their burrows under cover and close to sources of food and water. A typical rats' nest is actually fairly tidy. Starting with a 2- or 3-inch hole (usually just enough for one rat to pass at a time comfortably), the rat burrow goes about a foot deep before it opens up into the den. More like a living room really, the den is the common space where rats do much of their communal business. In the wild, the den is generally lined with plants, fur, and other soft debris to make it comfortable. In urban settings, these insulating materials have largely been replaced by shredded plastic bags, clothes, and newspapers. An exterminator from New York City told me he once found an intact teddy bear in a rat's sitting room, making me wonder if it was stolen from a sleeping child.

Of course, rats that live in sewers no longer need to burrow, but others do. They generally burrow as close as possible to food sources. Typically, they now burrow in piles of refuse in alleys (particularly close to restaurants and food stores), but any loose ground or debris will do. Rats can often be found in gardens, parks, and backyards. In January 1969, the *New York Times* reported rats in the most luxurious part of Manhattan—Park Avenue between 58th and 59th Streets, better known as the Silk Stocking District. It was a great leveler, democratically. While people had up until then believed that rats only lived in places like Harlem and the Lower East Side, they now knew that even the wealthiest New Yorkers were suffering from the same problem. What eluded the paper's editors and many of its readers, though, was that the rats they spotted were in the decorative planters mounted in the meridian between uptown-bound Park Avenue and downtown-bound Park Avenue, not in the homes themselves, which were, from most contemporary reports, largely rat free. Although rats can, of course, occur in even the most well kept homes, it doesn't happen very often. Similarly, I know a man who has stayed at the nearby Waldorf-Astoria hotel many times over the last twenty-five years and has repeatedly seen rats in the planters outside but never the slightest hint of one inside.

A number of intensive studies in the city of Baltimore led by James Childs, from the Center for Disease Control, indicated that rats are significantly more common in neighborhoods of lower socioeconomic status. One of the reasons that Ben, the exterminator from Brooklyn, postulates for this is that no matter how clean a person might be in a lower-income neighborhood, their neighbors and the common areas of their building—the lobby, the basement, the laundry, the garbage area—may not be. Higher densities of humans generally result in higher densities of rats.

Just as often in urban areas, rats will live protected under the concrete slabs of sidewalks or, especially in suburban areas, under porches and verandas where it's dark, there's no access for predators, and rats encounter few disturbances from humans. I looked at the homes the rats that lived in Ed's garage had made. The people who lived in the house before him stored newspaper, fiberglass insulation, and old clothes in cardboard boxes. They left behind a habitat so inviting they should have put out a neon sign saying "rats welcome here."

In most colonies, there are more tunnels and chambers. Often, the chambers are segregated by sex because males and females generally have little to do with each other except when mating and the threat of males committing infanticide is always present. Nests are sleeping chambers and are always insulated. Simple nests for individuals, also known as pads, are small and usually fit only one rat. Bigger nests are more complicated and can accommodate families or friends. The most luxurious are what rat experts call "hooded nests."

Usually made by a female rat to contain and protect her litters, they are sphere-shaped and elaborately lined. Hooded nests normally have just one, easily defended opening.

Larger colonies also have chambers dedicated to food storage. These larders are community property and rats can survive on them during times of duress—as when a hawk family moves into the neighborhood. Certain types of stored grain, when mixed with rat urine, can generate heat through fermentation and keep the entire underground colony warm in winter.

But no matter where rats live—a riverbank in Arkansas, a wharf in Hong Kong, a warehouse in Idaho, an alley in Toronto, a subway in Paris, or a sewer in Madrid—they always make sure that there's an escape route. At the back of every rat's nest is what experts call a "bolt hole." Normally well camouflaged—usually by leaves in the wild and newspapers or other refuse in urban areas—the bolt hole guarantees that the rats can escape if the front entrance is invaded by a predator. Some rat hunters I've spoken with take advantage of this. After finding the emergency exit, hunters will attack or disturb the main hole (the more dedicated of them will send a pet ferret or snake down the hole) then shoot the rats as they frantically exit the bolt hole.

Those bolt holes can become very busy when rats sense a larger danger. Since earthquakes can create havoc with burrows, collapsing even the best-built ones, rats head for the surface when they sense tremors. This phenomenon can be particularly alarming for people passing by a construction site as they can be unlucky enough to witness hundreds of rats pouring out of bolt holes when a jackhammer is being used.

Although listed biologically as herbivores, rats are true omnivores, eating pretty well everything they can get their paws on, but showing a distinct preference for protein-rich foods. Originally, rats depended a great deal on the water they lived by to provide much of their diet. They caught and ate fish, shellfish and insects in the water and lizards, salamanders and other small animals on land. Occasionally, rats tackled bigger game, especially any unattended young. They also enjoyed carrion, which was most often found on riverbanks as dead fish washed up or land animals tumbled down. When in season, wild rats appeared to have been especially fond of birds' eggs and nestlings. Of course, there was also a large vegetable portion to their diet. Rats ate fruit, berries, grain, and other plants. As with the animals they preyed upon, they tended to eat the youngest plants, feasting on tender seedlings as they emerged from the ground.

Now that most rats live with humans, their diet has changed considerably, but the basic elements remain the same. Rats generally eat a balanced diet with a distinct tilt towards protein. Studies in the field (for rats over the past hundred years or so, that often means alleys behind restaurants and food stores) have shown that urban rats' favorite food is not cheese or peanut butter but scrambled eggs. They have a distinct fondness for prepared foods, especially if they contain eggs, meat, or cheese. On the bottom end are raw vegetables, particularly tart or astringent ones like beets and peppers. Interestingly, while rats eschew raw potatoes, they readily consume french fries (especially those cooked in animal fat) or mashed potatoes if they are covered in cheese, butter, or gravy. The discovery of a McDonald's Sausage McMuffin with Egg and a side of hash browns would be like winning a lottery for a rat, although it would probably leave behind the parts of the muffin that weren't soaked in grease.

Ben, the Brooklyn exterminator, told me that there's an old saying in his business that if a rat were surrounded by raw vegetables and nothing else, it'd starve to death.

Commercially available pet-rat food is high in protein, and many rat owners feed young or thin rats puppy food in order to help them add bulk quickly. Although she's a vegetarian herself, Rat Fan Club president Debbie Ducommun found it impossible to make a meatless diet that would keep her rats healthy. British rat breeder Antonia Robinson recommends supplementing rat diets with "mealworms, lean meat or a dog biscuit every day." For a special treat, she points out

---

What, No Poodle?

Purebred varieties of rats recognized by the National Fancy Rat Society:

Standardized varieties

Agouti	Cinnamon	Roan
Badger	Cinnamon pearl	Russian agouti
Berkshire	Dumbo	Russian blue
Black	Essex	Russian blue agouti
Black-eyed Siamese	Himalaya	Russian dove
Black-eyed white	Hooded	Siamese
Blue agouti	Irish	Silver fawn
British blue	Lilac	Silvers
Buff	Lilac agouti	Squirrel
Burmese	Mink	Striped Roan
Capped	Pearl	Topaz
Champagne	Pink-eyed white	Variegated
Chinchilla	Platinum agouti	
Chocolate	Rex	

Source: National Fancy Rat Society

Argente crème?

Purebred varieties of rats recognized by the National Fancy Rat Society:

Unstandardized varieties

Apricot agouti	Coffee	Russian blue point
Argente crème	Cream	Siamese
Baldie	Havana	Russian silver
Bareback	Hooded downunder	Russian silver agouti
Black-eyed	Ivory	Sable Burmese
Himalayan	Merle	Satin
Blazed Essex	Platinum	Spotted downunder
Blue point Himalayan	Powder blue	Turpin
Blue point Siamese	Quicksilver	Wheaten Burmese

Source: National Fancy Rat Society

that rats enjoy "the odd cooked meat bone" and that chicken bones (which can't be fed to dogs or cats because they splinter into sharp shards) are not a problem.

Urban rats usually get their food from human refuse. Homes in which food scraps are carelessly left out overnight or improperly disposed of are the most likely to attract rats. Even the cleanest human dwellings can get rats if their food garbage isn't protected or if they compost in containers that aren't entirely rat-proof. From my own investigation, I've found that rats tend to congregate near the garbage containers for food stores and, especially, restaurants. Most large fast-food chains, like McDonald's, are very scrupulous about how they dispose of their food waste and, consequently, attract few rats despite how attractive their food is to them. McDonald's customers aren't always as neat as its employees, but since the restaurants' garbage cans are usually out in the open, they attract few rats. From my experience, the largest concentrations of rats are usually in the garbage-disposal areas behind small, independent restaurants (especially fast-food and greasy spoon–type diners), and supermarkets.

I found a perfect rat feeding ground in the alley just behind the stores and restaurants on the north side of St. Clair Avenue in Toronto near Bathurst Street that I went back to night after night. I sat there and waited, and before long, rats came crawling out from their holes—some in dirt, others in refuse—and started following what appeared to be familiar paths. The biggest rats seemed to come out first. The guy responsible for the garbage at one small market wasn't very careful and spilled a lot of it over the side. One rat sprinted to a cylindrical beef bone and began licking, then chewing on the marrow. When he couldn't reach it anymore, he started gnawing on the bone itself, making a new pathway to fresh marrow. Other rats ate different things and, true to what Ben the exterminator told me, I saw at least one rat walk over some raw lettuce, carrots, and what appeared to be spinach or Swiss chard on his way to the garbage receptacle. Although the big, rectangular waste bin had vertical painted metal sides about 5 feet high, the rats skittered up it with ease. Most took advantage of the attachments on the side that made the bin easier to lift, but some just took a running start and ran upwards. The garbage inside was piled pretty high, so getting out wasn't a problem. Many of the rats scrambled down the walls much like they had run up, but the bigger ones tended just to jump out and land where they may. All of the rats appeared almost to have a pre-assigned mission. None ever stopped to think about where it was going and none ever seemed to change its mind. There were rats who ate garbage lying around, those that made the pilgrimage to the great garbage can and others who went immediately to a pile of plastic garbage bags. The bags presented no difficulty to the rats, which expertly hacked them open with the nails on their front paws. Many of the rats brought food back with them to their holes, and the one that was sawing through the beef bone started dragging it back to the burrow before eventually giving up and entering some greasy cardboard boxes.

As long as I was sitting still, the rats didn't seem to mind me very much. If I moved, they all froze and remained motionless until they decided I wasn't really threatening them. If I did take a more aggressive approach, as in singling out an individual rat or rushing at the bunch of them, they all scrambled into the nearest safe spot and didn't emerge again until I backed off. Once they were confident I wouldn't attack them, they went back to the business at hand and gathered food. Interestingly, at the McDonald's a few blocks down, there were no rats at or near the garbage, although they did have a runway past it. The garbage there was sealed and the rats, apparently, either couldn't get in or preferred to find an easier meal.

One surprising thing I noticed was that the alley rats were significantly bigger than the pet rats I had met. They weren't any longer, just bigger around the rear end and midsection. Although obesity can be a problem with pet rats, the uncontrolled diets heavy in fats and sugars of wild rats and a lack of predation has appeared to make it rampant in the animals I observed. One particularly fat one I saw in the alley behind St. Clair did little other than lick at a yellowy-white slick of congealed cooking oil and was always the last to flee when I threatened them. This individual was so wide that I originally thought it was moments from giving birth to a huge litter, but when I identified him as a male, I realized he was just fat.

It's actually fairly easy to quickly identify the sex of rats. Males have a giant set of protruding testicles at the base of their tails. They're so obvious, in fact, that they have their own nicknames ("footballs," "goolies," and "torpedoes") among rat fanciers, and there's a Web site (ratballs.com, a division of a company named RatRaisins, itself a reference to a slang term rat owners use for their pets' droppings) devoted to them. "I thought the big pink bumps were repulsive," the owner of ratballs.com wrote on her site. "But as I had the boys for awhile, I found that I liked them. They're so full of character...and really excellent neck-warmers. I started thinking about male humans with their ratballs scaled to size." Male rats have enlarged testicles, a number of biologists have told me, because of their mating behavior. Big testicles are usually found on animals that engage in serial mating. When the female of a species mates with a large number of males, the males grow larger testicles to produce more sperm in an effort to make sure it's their sperm that gets to the egg. For animal species in which the females are more or less monogamous (and there are not many), testicle size is far less important. For example, a male gorilla usually mates with a high number of females who don't mate with any other males, which means his sperm has little if any competition. Consequently, a 400-pound gorilla's testicles are less than half the size of a rat's. The formula is so accurate that biologists will sometimes use testicle size to make educated guesses about a specie's mating behavior.

Even more important to a rat than food is water. Pet rats require fresh water and are best given it through ball-valve bottles. Although rats actually prefer to drink from a bowl, they have a habit of putting their food in them, which can rot and give off a bad smell. All of the wild rats I've watched drank frequently. Any bit of water was used, particularly small clear puddles on top of plastic or metal. The sewer rats drank only what appeared to be rainwater. Interestingly, I observed several different methods of drinking, with many older (at least larger) rats preferring to scoop water up with their paws and pour it into their open mouths. A biologist I spoke with told me that the rats who looked as if they were lapping up water with their tongues (like a dog or cat) were actually scooping it up with the backs of their top incisors.

Water is so important to rats that many people I spoke with in the pest control industry said that the most effective way to prevent a rat infestation and the first step in coaxing rats to leave is to cut off their water supply. Fixing a leaky faucet and putting the lid down on your toilet can help, but rats can get a surprising amount of moisture from licking the condensation off a toilet bowl or a cold-water pipe; and if rats are just entering your home in search of food, they can easily get their water from other sources.

Rats have to be very careful about what they drink, though. They are attracted to many human beverages because of their sugar (or artificial sweetener) content, but they're not all good for them. They very easily get drunk on beer or wine and their judgment, like our own, can quickly become impaired, with sometimes lethal consequences. More dangerous for rats, though, is soda. Because of an inability to belch, rats can suffer a great deal from gas buildup and can even die from just a little bit of Coke or Pepsi. Exterminators can't really take advantage of this because sodas tend to go flat before they can kill many rats.

Another thing I noticed about the rats in the alley that was different from those in the sewer is that they rarely made any noise. While the sewer rats were pretty confident in their chirping, the alley rats made no sounds that I could hear. A similar situation exists with coyotes, an opportunistic member of the dog family which has also adapted to human environments and now root through our garbage alongside rats and other animals. Although they are well known for their mournful howling, coyotes rarely if ever make any sounds in urban environments. The alley rats, however, weren't so much holding their tongues as communicating outside the range of human hearing, using the same high-frequency calls their ancestors reserved for such social interactions as sex and rough-and-tumble play. I could see them, often standing on their back legs, whipping their heads back with their mouths open. It was the same posture and motion the sewer rats assumed when they were chirping.

Much more of the rats' communication was non-verbal. When rats meet, they may give each other a whack, a bite, a grooming session, or one may crawl under the other or they may ignore each other entirely, all depending on their status within the colony. Rat colonies are male dominated. In areas of low rat population density, the rules are based on territoriality. Male rats entering into another male's territory act submissively, regardless of their size or ferocity. Conversely, that same rat would act dominantly and perhaps attack if another male were to enter his territory. Females, of course, are free to pass under any circumstances.

When rats live in closer quarters (at least one rat per 5 square meters), it becomes too difficult to enforce territorial boundaries, so males let it slide a little and boundaries overlap.

Male rats become hierarchical and when they meet, a strict stri-
ation of order emerges no longer based on the rat's location but
on the rat itself. Big rats who can win fights rise to the top, and
smaller or meeker rats sink to the bottom. Pet rats and those in
laboratory settings tend to live under the highest densities and
have the most despotic rulers. Sometimes, rats at the bottom of
the social order can become so submissive that they withdraw
from all interaction, then eventually from feeding and drinking. In a state not unlike human depression, lower-level male
rats can be so unwilling to do anything that they can die as a
result of their own inaction. Even if they don't withdraw
entirely, all submissive rats have higher mortality rates and
lower life expectancies than dominant rats.

Hierarchies are established early and rarely challenged.
As young male rats reach puberty, they feel out their peers to
find out where they stand and fight or submit as necessary
until they find their place. When there is some question as to
where a rat stands, the adversaries engage in what scientists
call agonistic behaviors. At first, the rats stand motionless,
sizing each other up and waiting for the other to make a
move. If neither backs off, they may engage in a series of
threatening behaviors. The combatants will bristle their fur,
gnash their teeth, arch their backs, and drum their feet. If
that display doesn't cause one rat to flee, the show escalates
as the rivals may paw at the ground like miniature bulls and
even stage mock charges.

When all avenues of non-contact combat are exhausted,
the rats lunge at each other. There are three basic types of rat-
on-rat fight. The most common is called a boxing match in
which both rats stand on their hind legs and pummel each
other with their forepaws. More serious encounters can lead to

a jump fight in which one or both aggressors jump at each other with all four paws extended. I've seen this happen. In the alley behind St. Clair there was one young male rat who would occasionally dive at his rivals kung fu–style, even though he was rarely challenged. The experts I asked about this behavior told me it was most likely a young male doing it simply for fun and was having a hard time finding any willing playmates. But he could have been trying to move up a notch in the colony's pecking order by bringing down some of his peers.

Even more serious than the jump fight is the wrestling match in which the fighting rats grab each other and roll around biting each other until one gives up. Fights like this almost always end with the retreat of one combatant, but he can be pursued by the victor and punished again to make sure he's really learned his lesson. The winner may bite the loser, usually on the testicles or rear end, and such pursuits usually end when the victor loses interest, although in the frenzy, he may attack another innocent rat who may be in his way. The overwhelming majority (88 percent in one extensive study in a Quebec landfill) of agonistic encounters ended in retreat.

If male rats from outside the colony approach, they are attacked by any available males. Since they almost always run away, intruders are rarely seriously injured. Once he leaves the colony's territory he's safe, as the aggressors will break off their attack as soon as he crosses the border. This behavior often leads to the establishment of new colonies as the chased-away male—perhaps playing the role of the handsome stranger—can attract young females and become the dominant male outside the borders of the established colony.

Interestingly, as I crossed St. Clair on my way home after my nights of rat watching, I would always pass through well-manicured Wells Hill Park into a somewhat more high-toned neighborhood. Once safely enveloped in the high-buck area, I noticed that the rat density had dropped to about zero. Every rustling in a garbage can turned out to be that of a fat raccoon family and every shaking hedge the result of a rummaging skunk. I'm not sure why this happened, but it may have been predation. Both raccoons and skunks will eat young, sick or infirm rats, as will the hawks, owls, and foxes that live in the ravine that cuts through the richer neighborhood.

While pet rats may live more than seven years, a wild rat is lucky if it lives a year. According to a number of studies conducted from 1948 to the present day, scientists generally agree that wild rats have an average mortality of 95 percent—meaning that an average of just 5 percent of rats survive to see their first birthday. In the wild, red-tailed hawks, owls, coyotes, and foxes take great numbers of young rats. Birds of prey have a great advantage over rats because their attacks—from behind and above and at great speed—are difficult to detect and usually result in a quick kill as the impact breaks the rat's neck or back. Urban rats are also run over by cars, poisoned, or trapped with great regularity. Although that may seem like a frightening number of deaths, it virtually always results in a large net gain of population because of the rat's early sexual maturity, large litter, and frequency of mating. It doesn't matter how often they're killed, there are always more rats.

Vermin School

In an effort to educate city workers about rats, the New York City Health Department opened the Rat Control Academy in 2005. "There's no question that we have a rat problem...the city has put out traps and poison at record rates," Mayor Michael Bloomberg said. Since a rat infestation in a public place can involve up to six different civic agencies, the school teaches all city workers how to deal with rats. Brooklyn-born rat expert Bobby Corrigan teaches a number of courses, most of which deal with rat myths and strategic rat control operations. "We don't have major rat infestations unless there's major food available," he said. "When people say 'How do I get rid of rats,' the first thing I always say is, 'Tell me what they're eating.' I don't say, 'Oh here's the poison.'"

Sources: Associated Press, New York City Public Health Department

Quagmire

Before you make a witty comment about the irony of a guy named Ben being a rat catcher, keep in mind that he's heard them all. Ever since the film *Ben* and Michael Jackson's ballad of the same name came out when Ben was five, he's had to put up with jokes about him being a rat, and it's only gotten worse since he became an exterminator in his twenties. "Yeah, I tried going by Benjamin for a while, but that was worse," he said. "At least when you introduce yourself as Ben, people get their comment out of the way upfront; but if you go by Benjamin, it comes out later, after they've made the connection, and they always feel like they're the first person to come up with it. It's better just to be Ben, otherwise I'd feel like I was hiding my name." It only gets to him now when his peers sing the song to him. "That totally sucks, because they think they're being funny and you don't wanna tell them that they aren't," he said. "It's the worst thing Michael Jackson ever did—at least to me."

He's also clear about the fact that he's an exterminator, even though the overwhelming majority of people in his profession abandoned that title for the term "pest control technician" more than a half century ago. "I hate that name— pest control," he almost spit as he said it. "It's like I run around herding rats through hoops and into cages or something." Ben is adamant that he doesn't control rats, he kills them. It kind of fits in with his personality. Ben is a big man, and looks more like a mastiff with his thick features and slow, deliberate movements than a rat terrier. He's a tough-looking guy with a cutting stare. Although he admits that the birth of his two children have lightened his outlook on life a little, he still speaks pessimistically, cynically, or fatalistically about most things. It doesn't come as a huge surprise that he's into a style of music he calls "death metal" and used to play in some "pretty nasty" bands himself.

Although he was born and raised in the Bronx (it sounds like "Brohngs" when he says it), Ben now works mostly in the nicer neighborhoods of Brooklyn (Carroll Gardens and Park Slope) and lives way out on Long Island. "You'll find that most exterminators live outside the city for the same reasons cops do," he said. "They see too much of the bad stuff to be able to put up with it." He knows there are rats out where he lives, but he knows their population densities are much lighter and that makes them much less aggressive. "The rats I see in the city would eat the guys out where I live," he said.

Ben is proud that he works for a private firm. "There's something not quite right about getting paid in taxpayer money unless you're a cop or a firefighter or something," he said. But he has a great deal of respect for the city's pest control officers, who have the unenviable task of ridding the city's housing projects and other facilities of some of the most horrifying infestations imaginable. "Those guys see the real shit," Ben said. He speaks of his pal Luis, who went into a subsidized apartment and found places where shredded paper, cloth, and other material were knee deep. "People don't do that," Ben pointed out. "But there were people in the residence—they were living with a pretty bold set of rats."

By comparison, the places Ben goes are posh. When he runs into rats, it's usually in the homes of the elderly or in buildings with very high turnover—like those that house students. Of the three most numerous pests he runs into ("the unholy trinity"), Ben considers cockroaches the most difficult. "Once you get cockroaches, it's murder to get rid of them," he said. He puts mice on the other end of the scale. "Mice are so stupid, it's almost like they want to die," he said. "If mice were the only problem in New York, everybody in the industry could be put out of business by a couple dozen cats."

Because most of the people who call him would rather not be associated with rats, he often has to be very discreet when he arrives. "I've actually had supers ask to meet me in a coffee shop or at a building around the block," Ben said. But when he meets the people who're paying for his services, he puts on a worthy show. When he arrives, he unloads dozens of snap traps, glue traps, live traps and mysterious-looking locked black boxes he calls bait stations.

Rat traps have been around for ages. Very little detail about the mundane elements of daily life from the medieval era has survived, but there was a metaphor that provides a description of rat traps in Chrétien de Troyes' romance *Yvain*, written about 1170:

This gate was very high and wide, but had such a narrow entry-way that two men or two horses could not
pass through together or meet one another in the gate
without crowding or great difficulty; for it was built just
like a trap that awaits the rat on its furtive scavenging:
it had a blade poised above, ready to fall, strike, and
pin, and triggered to be released and to fall at the slightest touch.

Even so, rats were rarely pursued by medieval Europeans
for reasons of cleanliness or health. It was a time of almost
unimaginable cruelty towards animals, and rats, familiar
and easy to catch, often suffered horrible fates simply for
amusement.

The first rat traps were, of course, cats. Armed with light-
ning-quick reflexes, sharp claws, and incredible stealth, cats
are excellent mousers but usually have trouble with rats, especially large brown rats. "Never get a cat to get rid of rats," said
Ben. "Cats hunt mice for fun, but hunting rats isn't much fun;
they're bigger, stronger, more aggressive and they'll gang up
on a cat." He then told me about his friend Luis, who had to
remove the remains of a treasured pet cat from a rat-infested
basement. "It's not fair, expecting cats to take on rats," Ben
said. "It's kind of like asking your family dog to kill a bear—
maybe he could do it, but is it really worth the risk?"

Even so, lots of people try to control rat populations with
cats, including many who should know better. When electric-
ity was brought into the tiny and remote Mexican town of
Atascaderos (loosely translated as "mud hole") in 2002,
many rats from the big city of Chihuahua followed the trail of
wooden poles into the town. Since Atascaderos's primary

industry is as a grain storage center, the rats found paradise. Before the year was out, the sleepy town of three thousand or so had a population of rats estimated by Mexican health officials at about 250,000. Desperate officials canvassed the citizens of Chihuahua for unwanted cats, emphasizing that since the rats came from the city, its residents were partly responsible. Although state pest control official Luis Martinez expected to assemble an army of at least seven hundred cats, he received just fifty. Not only didn't the cats make a dent in the rat population, many of them didn't survive their first winter in the harsh mountain climate.

Dogs are much better rat killers, but they have to have a desire to kill and most house pets simply don't. I've seen my own dog, Buckley, calmly watch as a mouse ate from his dinner bowl and he's been startled to the point of terror by rats that have suddenly popped out of garbage bags he was sniffing around. "Yeah, other than some terriers, it takes a mean dog to want to kill rats," said Ben. "Besides, who wants to see the food chain in action in their living room? When a dog kills a rat, it's not a pretty scene afterwards."

But like most exterminators, Ben doesn't expect to kill many rats with traps. "Mice fall for traps, but rats almost never do," he said, but he puts a few down anyway, just to prove he's doing his job. "I'm actually surprised these days whenever I catch a rat in a trap—sometimes I catch more squirrels than rats." The problem stems from two factors—the rat's innate neophobia (fear of the new), which makes it difficult to attract a rat to a trap in the first place, and the fact that rats, especially in places like New York where they have seen the same kinds of traps for hundreds of generations and have developed strategies to defeat them. Ben tells me he's seen rats expertly remove the bait off snap traps and jump right over glue traps. Usually, a well-fed rat (and most in cities are far from starving) simply bypass traps for more familiar foods.

The best way to entice rats to your trap is to bait it with their favorite food. Forget cheese and forget peanut butter ("that only works for mice," said Ben), rats have different tastes. For his landmark paper "A Preliminary Analysis of Garbage as Food for Rats," Martin Schein studied the eating habits of rats in the alleys, basements, businesses and schools of Baltimore. He found that the rats really enjoyed things like scrambled eggs, raw beef, macaroni and cheese, corned beef and fried chicken, while they disdained items like peaches, apples, cabbage, and carrots. When I presented him with Schein's lists, Ben nodded and agreed. "But he missed one thing. He missed their absolute favorite food," he said. "Bacon grease, it makes them crazy."

Every time he uses a trap of any kind, Ben uses bacon fat as the bait. To make it more enticing, he'll also smear bacon grease on and around the trap. The most commonly used devices are snap traps, which are larger versions of the classic mousetrap. Invented by Hiram Maxim, who is also responsible for the modern machine gun, the snap trap is deceptively simple in its operation and very economical. When a rat takes the bait from the trigger, it releases a spring-loaded bar which is intended to break the rat's neck. When using snap traps (usually along with other methods, as part of a much larger operation), most exterminators place them baited but unset in rat-infested areas. That method allows the rats a chance to get used to the traps and their baits, to make them visit the traps as a part of their daily food-finding routine. After this grace period, the human then sets the traps and hopes the rat will continue to visit their now-lethal bacon-fat dispensers.

Although they have proven somewhat effective over the years (especially for mice), snap traps have many drawbacks. They're very labor intensive. Since traps kill one rat at a time (and are unlikely to be reused once they do), there needs to be at least as many traps as there are rats (assuming a very unlikely 100 percent kill ratio). And anyone who's set a mousetrap knows how stressful it can be to pull back the bar, balance the trigger just so, and put the trap in place without setting it off. Of course, that tension is exponentially worse when setting a rat trap with its menacingly large bar and giant spring. While a mousetrap can give you a painful sting, a rat trap can easily break your finger. That bone-crunching power also means they must only be set in places children and other pets can't reach. Even so, untargeted kills are often a part of using snap traps.

Rats, perhaps sensing something's up or learning from the experiences of older rats, have become experts at defeating snap traps in some areas. Baits that are placed on the trigger (like cheese) can simply be delicately lifted off by the rat's sensitive front paws. Exterminators have tried to defeat this adaptation by gluing bait to the trigger (although the introduction of the scent of the glue can make the rats suspicious) or by using baits like chocolate or peanut butter that can be smeared on the trigger and can't be lifted off. But even that's no guarantee. "I've seen them lick the bait off the trigger right in front of me," said Ben. "But mostly they just ignore them. Snap traps really only have a chance when there's no other food around, and if there wasn't any food around there wouldn't be any rats in the first place."

Even when they do work, snap traps have another major drawback. Disposal of dead rats is never easy, and gloves must be used to prevent disease transmission, especially if blood, urine, or feces are present. "You'll usually get at least two out of three of those," said Ben. To ensure his clients' safety, he puts each rat corpse into a self-sealing plastic bag, then throws the bag into a cooler with a strong bleach-and-water solution for transport and eventual disposal.

Even more difficult are those times when the trap catches but does not completely kill the rat. "That's the worst, when you have a rat who's in the trap, but it's only just hurt and not dead," said Ben. "I've seen rats get caught by a foot or a tail and drag the trap all across a building. It's disgusting and pathetic at the same time." In those situations, it becomes the responsibility of the trapper to become an executioner, and a frightened and injured rat can be a very dangerous adversary. "That's the worst part of the job, when you actually have to kill something like that," he said. "I throw a bag over them and drown them—it takes a while sometimes." Ben claims never to have been bitten clearing a snap trap, but he's "come close a lot of times" and knows other exterminators who have. "It's pretty routine, you go to the E.R. and tell them you've been bitten by a rat," he said. "They give you some shots, tell you about some warning signs to look out for and you go back to work."

Since 1855, when Ralph Waldo Emerson uttered his well-known exhortation "Build a better mousetrap, and the world will beat a path to your door," people have been trying. The U.S. Patent Office issues about forty patents for new mouse-trap ideas every year and even has thirty-nine different categories—including "Impaling," "Smiting," "Choking or

Squeezing" and "Electrocuting and Explosive." And every year, many hundreds of mousetrap ideas are refused patents for being too derivative of existing traps or simply unfeasible.

One trap has succeeded to make a dent in snap-trap sales and even, for a short time, outsell them. Emerging commercially in the early 1980s, glue traps are amazingly simple, require no setting and are just as effective as snap traps at catching household pests. Available in mouse, rat, and snake sizes, glue traps are pieces of plastic or cardboard that are covered on one side with a super-sticky often nut-scented adhesive. Although some people bait them, placing one in a known runway is usually just as effective, especially for rats. When a rodent touches a glue trap, it gets stuck. If just one foot is stuck, the rodent will try to remove it with another, getting that one stuck and perhaps whiskers, tails, and other body parts.

The companies that sell glue traps say that the victim dies of exhaustion, but they are just as likely to die of starvation or dehydration. Struggling mice or rats often dislocate their joints or even break their limbs in their frantic attempts to escape. In most cases, the trapped animal is still alive (usually just barely) when the glue trap is discovered and that forces the person who finds the rat to make a decision about its fate. Sales of glue traps dropped precipitously as homeowners began to realize that if they followed the instructions on the traps, they were often throwing living, usually struggling and squeaking, mammals into their garbage cans. An old friend of mine, who was a strict vegetarian for what he called "moral reasons," had a Brooklyn apartment that was crawling with mice. Eventually he became frustrated enough to try glue traps. When I asked them how they were working, he said they were "catching lots of mice, but getting rid of them was hell." Seeing the poor animals covered in glue and twitching, he thought it was appropriate to euthanize them. Not realizing that the standard method was drowning—he was new to killing—he had been stepping on them until I set him straight. He admitted he would have handled the situation in an entirely different way (probably by moving to another building) had his opponents been rats.

Like snap traps, glue traps (also known as glue boards) are much more effective for mice than rats. Rats are simply too big and too smart to be caught as often. Although rats do sometimes plow into new objects placed in their runways, they are usually able to leap over glue traps when they smell one up ahead. And if disposing of a rat killed by a snap trap is gross and dangerous, getting rid of one on a glue trap is far worse. "I'm at the point now where I almost hope the glue traps don't catch anything," Ben said. "And most of the time they don't." It's possible to free a live animal from a glue trap with the use of mineral oil (which is poisonous and can end up killing the animal), but the desperate, confused victim is likely to bite (it will fight like the proverbial trapped rat) and is usually too severely injured to be released effectively.

Of course, there are traps designed to catch rats for live release. The most popular of them, from the beseechingly named Havahart company, is a wire cage that closes behind the animal when it enters the trap. Sturdy and reusable, live traps usually cost about twenty to thirty times more than a snap trap (which are about double the price of glue traps). Although they can be effective, especially in less urban areas, they have their own set of drawbacks. They must be checked frequently because rats can starve or dehydrate quickly, defeating the purpose of a live trap. And, as with all traps, disposal is a problem. Trapped rats need a place to be released. They are often brought to different environments than they are used to, which almost always has rats already. And if it doesn't, the live trapper is then releasing the most destructive of all animals into a potentially vulnerable environment. Historically, that hasn't been a good thing—saving the life of a single rat (especially a pregnant one) could result in the localized extinction of many plants and animals. Many humane societies will accept trapped rats, but they can't be adopted as pets and are likely to be euthanized.

There are other traps with various degrees of effectiveness. One man in Sweden told of a trap he devised and had remarkable success with, catching up to fifty-seven rats in a single day. He filled a bucket with a mixture of water and glycol (the main active ingredient in most types of antifreeze). He then put a baited wooden board on a swivel on top of the bucket and a wooden walkway smeared with bait up to the edge of the bucket. The baited board in the bucket was designed in such a way that if the rat stepped on it, it would tilt and the rat would fall face-first into the bucket. Although rats are excellent swimmers, they can't get any footing to escape from the slippery, poisonous water/glycol mixture and quickly drown. Traps of this type do work well in non-urban environments and rat expert Steve Belmain reports that the people he has worked with in Mozambique use similar traps involving holes dug in the ground, but they don't use poisons like glycol, which would render the rat inedible. Traps like this require a great deal of creativity and constructiveness and aren't legal in many places.

One of the latest rat traps on the market does show some promise. Electronic traps—the market leader is called the Rat

Zapper—use batteries to apply a high-voltage shock to the rat when it steps on the "killing plate." Death is almost always assured and immediate and some models have snap-shut doors and indicator lights so that the trapper "never has to see the dead rodent." Although expensive (about two or three times the cost of a live trap), electronic traps can be effective. Richie Ames, a warehouse manager in Jackson, Mississippi, told me that he used electronic traps with great success. "I tried everything else and still had rats," he said. "But the zappers took care of them—five the first day, and averaged about two or three a day after that." The problem with electronic traps, besides their initial cost and the batteries they require, is the rather complicated cleaning procedures necessary after a kill. It's so annoying, in fact, that the reusable traps many times end up being one-use only.

Electronic traps have had a hard time catching on with exterminators largely because of their high initial price and bad experience with another product they often associate with them. Many pest control companies offer electronic rodent repellents which use "ultrasonic waves" (sounds rats can hear and humans can't) to disturb, confuse, and annoy rodents. The main problem with them is that they don't work. In 2001, the Federal Trade Commission in the United States issued a warning to manufacturers and retailers of ultrasonic pest control devices that they would be investigated if they advertised claims that their products repelled pests, because there was no reliable evidence that they did. Even if they did have an effect on rats, the animals could get around it simply by traveling behind large objects, a sofa, for example, which they are prone to do anyway. Sadly, the electronic repellents can often have a more adverse effect on other animals, like pets or wildlife

(especially birds) within the target area. And with costs beginning at about six or seven times that of an electronic trap (or
many hundreds the cost of a single snap trap or glue trap),
ultrasonic repellents are not popular with many in the pest
control industry. "Those things are a scam," said Ben. "The
only time I've ever run into them in the field is when I walk
by them in the trash after I arrive to do the job right."

Doing the job right in most communities means using
poison. Humans have been attempting to keep pests away
from their possessions at least since the Sumerians started
sprinkling sulphur compounds around their crops to scare
away insects in 1500 BC. Poisoning rats, however, took longer
to emerge. Because of their ability to detect unsafe foods by
smell or taste, poisons had to be odorless and flavorless or at
least mimic the foods rats normally eat. Perhaps even more
important, poisons had to be relatively harmless to humans,
livestock, and pets.

The answer came from the poor soils on the northeastern
prairies. Around 1900, farmers in Wisconsin, Minnesota,
and Manitoba found the climate too harsh and soil too weak
to grow much for their cattle except for an extremely hardy
little plant called sweet clover. The cattle seemed to thrive on
the hay made from sweet clover until whole herds started
dying seemingly overnight without showing any outward
symptoms. Autopsies revealed that the cattle died of massive
internal bleeding. Word started spreading of the existence of
a "sweet clover disease," but scientists discovered in 1921 that
cattle only died when they consumed spoiled sweet clover. It
smelled and tasted the same as fresh sweet clover to the cattle, but contained a lethal poison called dicoumarol. After
World War II, there was a great deal of interest in the use of

dicoumarol as a rat poison, but it wasn't considered to be strong enough until 1948 when Dr. Karl Paul Link tinkered with it and discovered a potent rodenticide. To honor his benefactors, the Wisconsin Alumni Research Foundation, he used their initials in the name Warfarin. The similarity to the word "warfare" is not a coincidence.

It works very simply. In order to manufacture coagulants in the blood, mammals need to synthesize vitamin K. Warfarin effectively blocks the ability of the animal to absorb the vitamin and, without coagulants, the body has no way to stop internal bleeding. And it's perfect for rats. Odorless and tasteless, it can be mixed with almost any food and consumed. Since it can take many days (usually five) to kill, with no noticeable symptoms occurring until just before it kills, rats don't associate Warfarin with any ill feeling. Since rats don't recognize Warfarin as a threat, they will eat it repeatedly and share it with other rats in the colony.

Perhaps the best feature about Warfarin from a human perspective is its weakness in larger animals, especially with those, unlike rats and mice, who have the ability to vomit. In 1951, a sailor in the U.S. Navy tried to commit suicide by eating 20 ounces of Warfarin. After vomiting was induced and a blood transfusion administered, he recovered completely within a couple of days. Intrigued by the sailor's quick recovery, doctors investigated the use of Warfarin for human applications. Deemed far more effective in small doses than contemporary anticoagulant medicines used in humans to fight circulatory complications, Warfarin went on the pharmaceutical market in 1954. President Dwight Eisenhower was treated with the drug later that year after he suffered a mild heart attack. With his tacit approval, Warfarin's commercial success as prescription drug was guaranteed. It's still widely prescribed around the world.

Warfarin was very effective, killing millions of rats over the decades, but became a victim of its own overuse. After hundreds of generations of exposure to Warfarin, rats developed a resistance and then outright immunity to the poison. Before long, exterminators began to notice that their poisons didn't seem to have the kick they had just a few years earlier and started using bigger and stronger doses. Warfarin-resistant rats first showed up in clinical tests in Scotland as early as 1960. Tests carried out in the United States in 1976 revealed that Warfarin had little or no effect on 12 percent of rats in New York City and 65 percent of rats in Chicago, with the most resistant rats in lower-income neighborhoods. By the 1980s, most rats could enjoy Warfarin snacks with little or no ill effects. Rats who lived in big cities, who generally saw Warfarin more often and bred faster, developed immunity quicker. "I think it's an absolute travesty that they still sell Warfarin in stores in New York, pretending it will kill rats," said Ben. "If you buy it, you're really just buying your rats a free meal."

With Warfarin's effectiveness sagging, rodenticide manufacturers have come out with a second generation of anticoagulants. The most popular of them is brodifacoum, marketed under the names Final, D-Con, Talon, and Havoc. It's what Ben uses, and what professional rat catchers I've spoken to from as far way as New Zealand, the Falkland Islands, Japan, and Scotland use.

The most important weapons at Ben's disposal are his bait stations. Black plastic rectangles about as big as a shoe box, the bait stations have a locking lid on top and a small hole at one

of the bottom sides. He prefers to use the Protecta boxes, man-
ufactured by Bell Labs, but doesn't give any specific reason
other than familiarity. He values a good bait station because
Final is potentially much more dangerous to humans and non-
target animals than Warfarin ever was. He always keeps his
stations as out of the way as possible (rats prefer those spots
anyway) and securely locked. "I don't want some kid going to
the hospital because of me," he said. He also smears bacon
grease on the poison pellets and around the entrance.

Even when he's only placing traps, Ben always wears
Kevlar gloves. Using the same lining as bullet-proof vests, the
gloves never come off when he's at work. He also tucks his
pant legs into his steel-toed boots and his shirt into his pants
and his sleeves into his gloves. When he's finished with those
precautions, he puts on a surgical-style mask and is ready to
work. He's just heard too many stories not to suit up properly
before every attack. "It's not just the bites; you hear about a
guy in the industry who's died of this cancer or that," Ben
said. "They can say it's unrelated to the job all they want, but
I'm not going to take those chances."

Poison isn't as messy as trapping, but dead rats are still
dead rats. Luckily for most homeowners, the first symptom a
rat feels when poisoned with an anticoagulant is sudden and
massive dehydration. Usually, that desperate thirst sends
affected rats out of their home buildings in search of sources
of water. Ben has seen rats in the final stages many times.
"It's almost sad really, when the rats get stupid," he said (he
uses the word "stupid" a lot). "You see them coming out,
walking slow, and out in the open, they don't even notice people around them, it's like they're charmed." Many in the
business call the last stages of a poisoned rat's life "dead rat

walking," but Ben finds that a bit flip. He prefers to call it "the rattaan death march."

An added benefit of anticoagulants is that they are so good at dehydrating a rodent that it almost mummifies their bodies, holding decay to a minimum. If death occurs within the building, the smell is nowhere near as bad as that of a normally decomposing rat and goes away entirely in two to four weeks.

As effective as brodifacoum and its competing anticoagulants have been, it may be time to start looking for a new poison again. In 2004, a pig farmer in the northeastern part of Yorkshire, England, not far from where the first Warfarin-resistant rats were found in Scotland, noticed that the number of rats on his land appeared to be increasing despite the intense application of brodifacoum. He called the British Department of Environment, Food and Rural Affairs, which was especially interested after finding out that the Pest Technicians Association in the area had reported a 17 percent increase in rat-related calls over the previous two years. Clinical tests showed that many of the rats taken from the farm were highly resistant to brodifacoum. The BBC quickly named them "super rats." When similarly resistant rats were found in Tokyo, Hiromi Kanemaru's book *Super Rats, the Horror of the City Beasts* quickly became a best-seller. Atascaderos, the beleaguered Mexican town that tried cats and other methods (including something called "magic molasses") to get rid of its rats, were further frustrated when it was determined that many of their rats were also brodifacoum resistant.

The emergence of the so-called "super rats" indicates that poison will always be, at best, a temporary solution. While science can probably continue to come up with more lethal poisons, there are always prices to be paid. The anticoagulant concept may soon come to an end as more and more baby rats are born with immunity. Other poisons can and have been used on rats (including such terrifying concoctions as strychnine and arsenic) but they can put non-targeted animals in grave danger and can have long-term environmental consequences.

A lesson can be learned from the pest control industry. In 1948, Swiss chemist Paul Hermann Müller won the Nobel Prize for Physiology or Medicine for his work in developing dichloro-diphenyl-trichloroethane (better know as DDT). At the time, it was hailed as a wonder chemical, saving millions of human lives by, among other things, controlling mosquito populations in malaria-afflicted countries.

But by 1962, the adverse environmental effects of DDT, including driving many species of birds of prey to the verge of extinction, became well known and conclusively proven. By the early 1970s, most countries had banned DDT, and many affected bird populations have only started beginning to come back about a quarter century later. As DDT-laden insect larva were eaten by fish, the fish were in turn eaten by ospreys and bald eagles. While the levels of DDT accumulated were not enough to kill the birds, it thinned the shells of their eggs to the point where very few survived long enough to hatch. Similarly, the Sierra Club in California has reported that many predators, particularly bobcats and foxes, are dying of complications directly linked to brodifacoum poisoning developed from eating poisoned rats.

A 2003 rat infestation in the National Zoo in Washington, D.C., led employees to make their own attempts at pest control. They began with snap and glue traps, then moved to commercially available poisons. When those methods didn't kill many rats, they resorted to arming volunteers with BB guns. When that didn't work, they hired a professional pest control agency. The exterminators used brodifacoum and did a pretty good job at reducing the zoo's rat population. They did, however, make a big mistake. The exterminators accidentally dropped a few poison pellets into some animal exhibits. Two rare red pandas died and, after a long and costly court battle, the pest control firm was fined $2000.

The current trend in rat poison research is not in newer forms of anticoagulants, but in sterilization. By making male rats incapable of producing sperm, the new baits prevent new litters—in theory. In practice, so far, sterilization baits have proven largely ineffective. While many male rats have doubtless had their sperm made impotent, the concept is largely defeated by the fact that most female rats mate with every male rat in the colony. If the local males prove unable to reproduce, females can draw suitors from up to 10 miles away. Even if such baits could make every rat in a 10-mile radius incapable of fathering young, they would still be subject to the same limitations of other baits—taste and smell appeal and acquired immunity.

Of course, it's not really safe (or desirable) to live with wild rats. But since trapping isn't all that effective and poisoning becomes less so with each generation of pinkies, it may appear that rats have won the war against humans. But I know one man who doesn't believe it and is trying to spread the gospel. Joe Luzi's official title is south district manager for Toronto Municipal Licensing and Standards, which means he's the guy who hears about everything bad with every house and apartment building in the most densely populated part of the city. His job is to handle complaints about rotted beams, leaky roofs, strange smells, cockroaches and, especially, rats. Despite the fact that his job brings him into conflict constantly, he's very plain-spoken and it's pretty easy to get an opinion from him. And his opinion on rats is that whether you're trapping or poisoning them, you're applying a solution after the problem's already gotten out of hand. "The secret to staying rat free is to keep them from getting in your building in the first place," he said. "To keep rats out, make sure you don't leave any food around and, even more important, deny them a constant water supply."

Since rats need to drink regularly, water is, as we have seen, key to controlling them. According to studies conducted by Patrick D. Warrington, a scientist with the British Columbia Ministry of Environment, Lands and Parks, rats need about ten times as much water as mice or gerbils. The theory is that if you cut out the water, the rats will probably look for somewhere else to live. Similarly, the Saskatchewan Ministry of Environment exhorts farmers to: "Immediately bury spoiled and treated grain, elevator cleanings and dead animals." Burning these items, though legal in the province, can actually increase rat populations. "Rats tend to be attracted to waste disposal grounds by smoke from burning refuse," reads a line in one of their rat-prevention guides.

Equally as important is denying rats entry into your home. They crawl into buildings through all kinds of holes or other access points. "You may also want to inspect your house for access points," said Luzi. "Small rats can squeeze in through a hole the size of a pencil." He suggested stuffing steel wool into any holes that can't be sealed with plaster or caulking. Of course, a determined rat can gnaw through plaster, caulking or steel wool (or even through the bricks your house is made of), but as Ben sees it, rats are rarely all that determined. "They're opportunists, they're like car thieves," he said. "As soon as they see that your building is a little more difficult than the building next door, they're going to go next door."

Although Luzi acknowledged that rats do appear more often in low-income neighborhoods, people in nicer places shouldn't think they couldn't get rats. "I've often seen them in apartment complexes because there's food and refuge in common areas," Luzi said. "But single-family dwellings in high-income neighborhoods can attract rats, too, especially in backyards." The problem is usually just that the homeowner isn't thinking about what attracts rats because he or she doesn't think rats can happen in their neighborhood. "An old woodpile or boards can supply a home for rats," Luzi said. "And a poorly sealed composter or an unprotected bird feeder can provide food."

"Don't Take Are Rats"

Sample from the online petition to stop the proposed ban of pet rats by the Saskatchewan government:

CANADA IS THE WORST COUNTRY ON THE FACE OF THE EARTH! ARE THEY CRAZY!?BAN RATS? THAT'S RUBBISH!!!!

Source: petitiononline.com

Future Rat

E verybody knew I'd want to see the giant rat. It was a nice early summer day in 1989 and I had just finished up my show on the college radio station when a couple of my friends came running into the office screaming about the giant rat that they'd found in the woods just off campus. It was as big as a cat, they said while trying to catch their breath. It was bigger than a cat. It was as big as a raccoon. It was huge.

The students at McMaster University in Hamilton, Ontario, are lucky enough to have a diverse, if not pristine, natural habitat just to the north of the main campus. On the south shore of a marshy body of water called Cootes Paradise, the thick deciduous forest is home to many kinds of wildlife including muskrats, skunks, red foxes, and white-tailed deer. Every so often, students will hike into the woods with a lunch, some beer or, just as often, a few joints. I'm not sure what my friends were doing down there, but when they saw the giant rat, Rob and Cameron came running to get me and Brian was left in the woods to make sure it didn't get away.

When we got there, Brian was sitting among a few empty beer bottles. Still excited, he pointed into the oak tree where the giant rat was. It was big, not exactly as big as a cat, but much bigger than any rat I'd ever seen—about as big as a loaf of Wonder Bread. As I approached, it showed its pointy teeth and hissed at me. It was covered in scraggly gray fur, had a pointy snout, and a long, naked tail. Like all reports of giant rats that aren't exaggerations or outright fabrications, this one was a case of mistaken identity. My friends had managed to corner an opossum. Outwardly, opossums (North America's only native marsupial) look very much like giant rats. And, like rats, they have benefited by the presence of humans and expanded their population and range as humans have changed the landscape—although on a much smaller scale than rats. As little as sixty years ago there were probably no opossums in Canada, so it's not surprising that pretty well every time one of the lumbering beasts is spotted in a back-yard there, the local humane society gets a frantic call about a giant rat.

For some reason, people love to talk about the idea of giant rats, as though having lived through the experience of larger rats than anyone else confers some kind of toughness or savoir faire upon them. Whether I'm in New York, Toronto, or any other large city, when people find out I write about rats, they seek me out to tell me their rat stories. Most are interesting, but I generally discount the ones about gargantuan rats. Of course, rats, like all widespread mammals, do vary in size. Generally the more northern an animal it is, the bigger it is. This is out of necessity as rats in colder places need more fat and a bigger size to skin-area ratio to stay alive. Obese pet rats and non-commensal species aside, rats vary from somewhat less than a pound in the tropics to somewhat more than a pound in the Arctic, although thicker fur can make them look bigger. In the 2003 version of the film *Willard*, the part of Ben (the rat commander) was played by a Gambian pouched rat. About double the length and six times the weight of a brown rat, Ben certainly stood out amongst his peers; but whether he made the film scarier or not is up for debate. Other than a robust 17.5-incher posted on Ratkill.com, the biggest brown rat I've ever seen probably weighed a bit less than 2 pounds. I was in the parking lot of a small Toronto supermarket on an overcast November afternoon when I heard an oddly rhythmic clicking noise. The source of the sound was a big, tawny rat who'd climbed out of a garbage can and was headed towards another. The tapping actually came from his claws hitting the pavement as he sauntered over to the new can, seemingly much less disturbed by my presence than I was by his.

But bigger may not necessarily mean better as far as rats are concerned. As a prey species in the wild and an enemy to most humans, rats prefer to be as inconspicuous as possible. Bigger species of rats, like the bandicoots of India, tend to be slower moving than their smaller cousins and run the risk of increased detection and death. Natural selection, then, would appear to favor rats stay about the same size they are.

But rats have undergone some adaptations that help ensure their continued success in a human-dominated world. Of course, some behavioral changes like the learned ability to lick peanut butter off the triggers of snap traps and how to negotiate around glue traps has been acquired in just the last century or even more recently. Far more profound than what rats have learned and passed on have been the immunities they have developed to our poisons. "Britain is under siege from an emerging breed of rat that is not vulnerable to any present-day poisons," said John Davison, of the U.K.'s National Pest Technicians Association. "Not only have the rodents developed resistances to previously deadly anticoagulants, but they have been learning from other rats to avoid the poisons after witnessing their effects." That's actually not new, but in just the half-century since humans have been using anticoagulants to kill rats, they have grown immunity to them twice. It probably doesn't matter if we do develop better rodenticides, because rats are getting more resistant to our poisons; they're getting smarter about them too.

Humans are constantly striving for more effective poisons that neophobic rats will eat. Of course, this prevents other dangers. As rat poisons become more noxious, they present greater dangers to non-rat species as well. Domestic animals and even children frequently ingest poisons intended for rats, and deaths have resulted. Rat poisons have been used for suicide attempts and as murder weapons for centuries—usually with ineffective results. Old-school poisons like Warfarin were usually easy to detect and accidental or intentional victims were usually effectively treated with emetics. But as new, more complex poisons are available, the stakes have been raised. In September 2003, a restaurateur in Tangshan, China, was so jealous of the business his rival was enjoying at the Heshengyuan Soy Milk snack shop, he hired a disgruntled cook to sprinkle rat poison (most likely brodifacoum) over the café's breakfast offerings. Within a week, forty diners were dead and more than three hundred hospitalized. A similar incident occurred a month later in Lichaun City, killing eleven.

One side effect of the war on rats has been an increase in the number and size of accidental discharges of increasingly virulent rat poisons into vulnerable environments. On May 29, 2001, a truck carrying rat poison on a seaside road near Kaikura, New Zealand, was involved in a head-on collision with another vehicle. The entire load from the truck—almost 20 tons of rat poison—spilled into the surf. Tests conducted by the company that made the poison and the New Zealand government who bought it showed no signs of toxicity in whales, dolphins, or birds in the area, but trace amounts of the poison did end up in shellfish, many of which are eaten locally. "The loss of a contaminant like this into the environment is of extreme concern," said Bob Simpson, a regional enforcement officer with the New Zealand Environment Agency. "Thankfully, from the results to hand, the impact appears to have been minimal."

While we try our best not to kill other animals and ourselves in our attempts to poison rats, we often help them in other ways without realizing it. Rats thrive in the conditions created by tragedies and war, often feeding on unattended food and even corpses and enjoying life more or less unmolested among the chaos as humans do everything they can to save themselves and their loved ones. Rats can't (as a surprising number of people believe) survive a nuclear blast, but thanks to their simple structure, they suffer less from radiation than humans—a fact exploited frequently by science-fiction writers who like to populate post-apocalyptic worlds with swarms of angry and even vengeful rats. The first mammals to return to the worst affected areas of Hiroshima and

Nagasaki after the atomic bomb blasts there, rats are, in essence, better prepared for the effects of nuclear war or accident than we are.

It would appear then that rats are perfectly suited to living in a world that is otherwise dominated by humans. We can't kill them quickly enough and neither can the animals we hire to do the jobs for us. Our traps aren't very effective and our poisons are becoming impotent—we can't even nuke them. But what will happen to rats in the future, perhaps after we're gone? To find out, I asked Robert McNeill Alexander, a biology professor at the University of Leeds in England and a man whose job it is to make extremely well-educated guesses about what will happen to animals in the future. He was a leading contributor to "The Future is Wild," a highly rated television program that featured possible scenarios of wildlife, often millions of years from now. Although he made it clear that he couldn't actually predict what would happen, he did speak of possibilities. Realizing that the rat's diet is increasingly carnivorous, he indicated that the rat's teeth could become even more fearsome. He said he could see it "using its incisors as weapons or with venom glands at the bases of the incisors." These bigger, badder teeth could have other uses. "There are possibilities for a variety of social systems," he said. "And for the incisors to become tusks with a function in inter-male conflict."

While the thought of a poisonous, saber-toothed rat might seem too horrible to contemplate, keep in mind that many of the changes we've seen in rats—the learned behaviors, the resistance to poison and the conquering of new habitats—have occurred over hundreds of years, not the usual millions we normally associate with evolutionary change. In the same time it has taken humans to create great civilizations, architecture, and other works or art while scarring the landscape, polluting the water, and befouling the air, the rat has come along for the ride and ably, if not nobly, has gone everywhere we have—even outer space. While humans appear to be intent on driving every other competitor to extinction, the rat has quietly adapted to our every move. But while rats haven't gotten any bigger and they haven't grown poisonous fangs or tusks, they have seen an outstanding amount of success. It would appear that for a human-dominated world, they're already perfect.

Of course, it doesn't take a genius to see that the rat's story is a disturbingly familiar allegory of our own. Rats started small and only a few thousand short years ago they were struggling for their very existence with the other competitors in swamps while we were duking it out with the other big predators on the grasslands. But then these animals started living together for mutual safety and to gather enough food so that their increasingly large omnivorous colonies fed during hard times. They made elaborate homes and developed social structures that simplified their lives and ensured that important genetic material was spread around, further guaranteeing the survival of the group. They learned ways to protect themselves from their enemies and from the poisons in their environment. They have been so successful that they number in the billions and occur in every country in the world.

But the flipside of their almost unprecedented success has been the destruction they've caused. Rats have transformed a large number of islands into wastelands barren of any other animal life. They have been responsible for the extinction of hundred of species of plants and animals and the regional extirpation and endangerment of many more. They have killed plenty of their own kind and millions of ours. They destroy their habitat and environment, while breeding at a rate that seems ridiculous when compared to what the world will actually sustain.

But there is one significant difference between rats and humans—restraint. At least some humans have foreseen and acknowledged the limitations of their world. Through the use of things like contraceptives, recycling, lands set aside as parks and reserves and pollution controls, humans have at least tried to slow their destruction of the earth. While it would be too ambitious an effort in anthropomorphication to think that rats can comprehend their effect on the planet, it's clear that their destructive spread must be curtailed. Human intervention can limit their effect on the planet—just as it unleashed it a few centuries earlier.

With a mind-set dedicated not to the violent extermination of commensal rats, but rather a widespread practice of measures that deny rats food, water, and shelter, humans can limit rat populations and the amount of destruction their little partners can commit. When Steve Belmain convinced the farmers he met in East Africa to take a few simple preventive measures against, rats like covering water vessels and clearing the area around their houses of ground cover, local rat populations fell precipitously. Of course, a large-scale plan of action would require a massive worldwide rebuilding of homes, sewers, farms, businesses, and other infrastructures. Until something like that could happen, rats and humans are perhaps unwilling partners in an ever-increasing upward spiral of population and destruction.

But it's often hard for humans to fight their baser urges when it comes to rats. Although it may be more effective to get rid of rats by denying them a place to live and sustenance, it is, for most people, more satisfying to kill them. As barbaric as that sounds to those in what they believe to be rat-free environments, it's an urge almost impossible to deny by those forced to live among them. For just a few months, I voluntarily entered the world of rats—the basements, garages, stores, alleys, and sewers—and always knew I'd be coming out the other side into a (as far as I knew) rat-free life. But even so, after being among them, I found myself constantly thinking about rats, seeing them in the shadows and around every corner and having rat-themed dreams. Once, when somehow encountering my own hand under my pillow, I leapt from a sound sleep, convinced I'd touched a rat. When my sons were playing a sloppy game of football in the park across the road from our house, I saw a movement in the wet leaves. Without thinking, I positioned myself between it and the boys and was ready to pounce on it with my bare hands. Luckily, the intruder turned out to be the far end of a long fallen branch my son had stepped on.

I can only imagine what it's like for people who have to live with rats and have no easy escape route and, often, no end in sight. Everybody I talked to—researchers, exterminators, health inspectors, farmers, business owners, homeowners, and tenants—said the same thing: "You never get used to them." The only exceptions to the rule were the sewer workers, who left their rats behind after every shift. And pretty well everyone I spoke with wanted to see the rats they came into contact with dead, not merely moved onto someone else. Despite never having lived anywhere but big cities and

sometimes having less than exemplary hygienic standards, I have never had to live with rats, at least as far as I've known. What I do know about rats I know from invading their world or from talking with those who have no choice but to put up with them. But despite my ability to withdraw from the rats' world, I know that if I saw one in my kitchen, I'd want it dead, not relocated to some less fortunate guy's house.

Ben, the exterminator, is particularly suspicious of any plan to get rid of rats that doesn't involve their death. "Starving them out doesn't get rid of rats, it only moves them onto a less disciplined building—there's always someone a bit messier, a bit less organized than you are," he said. "Even if you manage to get everybody up to the same level of cleanliness, rats won't starve—they'll just get more desperate. Instead of living in your basement, they'll live in your cupboards. I wouldn't be surprised if they eventually learned to open the fridge."

Acknowledgments

At first he didn't like the idea. But one of the great things about Rick Haliechuk is that he'll let you argue your point and sometimes you can convince him that you know what you're talking about. Rick's an editor at the *Toronto Star* and he'd printed a few of my articles about rattlesnakes and coyotes, but he wasn't sure he wanted one about rats. Sure they were animals, but were they part of nature? Did anybody want to read about them?

Apparently, they did. The article, "Teeth like steel, able to swim in sewers, the brown rat has long plagued humans," drew more comments than all of the hundreds of articles I had ever written combined. While a few pet-rat owners and animal rights activist types were up in arms about how I portrayed rats as villains, most people just wanted to tell me their rat stories. It wasn't only my friends in Toronto and New York, but people I knew in smaller communities and in places like England, Jamaica, and Uzbekistan. Word spread and soon the manager of the liquor store in my neighborhood

was telling me about the rats he'd seen when he was in the Hungarian army. Finding material was easy. Nobody, it seemed, had lived a life without somehow coming into contact with rats.

A few weeks later, I had just gotten back from the M3 music and multimedia festival in Miami Beach when my wife told me that a woman kept calling, asking me to get in touch with someone named Anna Porter. I didn't think much of it—perhaps it was just another angry rat owner—but eventually called. Anna Porter turned out to be *the* Anna Porter, the then-boss of Key Porter publishing. Apparently, she'd read the article and was so impressed—or creeped out—that she thought it would make a good book. I agreed.

When the book actually started to happen, the new boss at Key Porter was a guy named Jordan Fenn. We were supposed to have a 30-minute meeting about the book and it turned into a couple of hours. Not only did he have an outstanding handle on the idea, but he was also smart, creative, insightful, and enthusiastic. Before the meeting, I kind of wanted to make the book, afterwards, I couldn't wait. Just talking to him made the book better. An author, especially one who isn't entirely cynical about the process, could not ask for a better, more creative publisher.

Luckily, Fenn was the spearpoint of a spectacular team at Key Porter. If you like *Rat*, thank editor Jonathan Schmidt— the guy knows how to make a good book, and he brought *Rat* up to where it is. The rest of the Key Porter people—senior designer Marijke Friesen and most notably Marnie Ferguson, Sheila Evely, Kendra Michael, Carol Harrison, Sandra Homer, Michelle Welsh, and copyeditor Liba Berry—also did an outstanding work and made this book happen. Likewise,

they probably never would have gotten much to work with if it weren't for the tireless and incredibly professional help of my great friend and agent, B.G. Dilworth.

The book itself comes from the experiences of people who live with rats or work with rats and, unlike me, don't really have the option of putting rats behind them. From Ed, the homeowner who had a rat jump into his hood; to Ben, the self-described "rat terminator", to Ang and his crew in the sewer; to Ryan, the beleaguered corn farmer, it was the people who live day in and day out with rats, the people who are on the front lines of our war against them, that made this book possible. Perhaps even more important are the people like Steve Belmain, Darren Christie, and Pete McClelland who are leading the fight against the destruction rats commit against people and nature.

For this book I am also greatly indebted to the greatest of the great, Herbert S. Zim, who has inspired me every day since I was five, and my brother Mark, whose brutal honesty keeps me from being more of a goofball than I am. Most of all, though, I have to thank Tonia, Damian, and Hewitt—the collective reason for everything I do.

About the Author

JERRY LANGTON is a freelance journalist who frequently writes for *The Globe and Mail* and the *Toronto Star*. In doing research for *Rat*, Langton ventured into the sewers and alleys to meet the infamous rodents face to face.

He lives—relatively rat-free—in Toronto.